Coping
with
Depression

"Tan and Ortberg have written an exceptionally comprehensive yet readable book on managing depression. The combination of clinical wisdom and biblical insight will be helpful to people struggling with depression or to those working with them. For years this text was a student favorite in my pastoral counseling classes—and the second edition is even better!"

C. Jeffrey Terrell, Ph.D., president, Psychological Studies Institute

"If depression is the common cold of the emotional life, then this volume reveals the cure. With this concise guide, psychologists Tan and Ortberg unravel the complex theories, research, and treatments for depression. Writing with a striking blend of compassion and authority, the authors guide us into the dark chamber of clinical depression and then show us to the exits.

"The authors clearly describe how depression can be effectively managed and overcome with a rich mix of emotional, cognitive, behavioral, and spiritual tools. Combining state-of-the-art psychological interventions with biblical wisdom, this book is certain to become a source of insight and change for the many souls among us needlessly bearing the burden of depression."

W. Brad Johnson, Ph.D., associate professor of psychology, United States Naval Academy

Coping
with
Depression

Revised and Expanded

Siang-Yang Tan and

John Ortberg

BakerBooks
Grand Rapids, Michigan

© 2004 by Siang-Yang Tan and John Ortberg

Published by Baker Books
a division of Baker Publishing Group
P.O. Box 6287, Grand Rapids, MI 49516-6287
www.bakerbooks.com

Printed in the United States of America

Library of Congress Cataloging-in-Publication Data
Tan, Siang-Yang, 1954-
     Coping with depression / Siang-Yang Tan and John Ortberg—Rev. and expanded.
          p.   cm.
     Includes bibliographical references.
     ISBN 0-8010-6491-0 (pbk.)
     1. Depressed persons—Religious life. 2. Depression, Mental—Religious aspects—Christianity. I. Ortberg, John. II. Title.
BV4910.34.T36 2004
248.8′625—dc22   2004006529

To Angela,
and to my mother, Madam Chiow Yang Quek
and the memory of my late father, Siew Thiam Tan.

Siang-Yang Tan

To Nancy
and to my father and mother,
John and Kathy Hall Ortberg.

John Ortberg

Contents

Acknowledgments

We would like to acknowledge, with deep gratitude, the help of Kim Roth, secretary to Siang-Yang Tan at the Graduate School of Psychology, Fuller Theological Seminary, as well as the support and interest provided by Dr. David Benner, and by Paul Engle and Maria den Boer of Baker Book House, in the first edition of this book. Special thanks to Simon Reeve-Parker, assistant to Siang-Yang Tan at Fuller Theological Seminary, for his excellent work and help, and to Donald Stephenson and Mary Wenger of Baker Book House for their interest and support in the second edition of this book.

We would also like to express appreciation and love for our dear children Carolyn and Andrew Tan, and Laura, Mallory, and Johnny Ortberg, whose patience and love (and interruptions) made the writing worthwhile and kept us from getting depressed!

Most of all, we want to thank God for his help and blessing as we wrote this book together, and for the depth of Christian fellowship and spiritual direction that we experienced in Christ as we worked and prayed together. We trust and pray that this book will be a real help and blessing to its readers.

1

A Snapshot of Depression

The "Common Cold" of Emotional Life

He had everything going for him.

He was a preacher of national renown. He interacted regularly with people at the highest echelons of power. The impact of his ministry was widely recognized by his peers and even by leaders of other religious traditions. His work had faced severe challenges, at times from powerful opponents, and yet somehow he had always continued. His personal integrity was unchallenged. His spiritual life was impeccable, at least to all appearances. He had seen answers to prayer that were nothing short of miraculous. His moral character was untainted by scandal. He not only had distant admirers but was also capable of close personal relationships and intimate partnering with colleagues in ministry. His assertiveness skills and willingness to confront head-on were legendary. He had just experienced a time of great success in his ministry, one of the peak moments of his career.

And he was depressed.

He withdrew, not only from his ministry, but from all his relationships. His loss of energy and motivation went far beyond the bounds of normal burnout; he was no longer able even to connect emotionally with other people. His perceptions became distorted; he really believed that who he was and what he had done lacked any redeeming value at all. He felt isolated and abandoned, and was certain that nobody supported him in his life's work. He was in a state of fatigue: both his appetite and sleep patterns were disrupted. His emotional mood was extremely low: he berated himself and believed he was no longer able to make a significant contribution to life. He was consumed by fear and a sense of hopelessness. In fact, his will to live had largely eroded, and he wanted to die.

His name was Elijah.

The pages of the Bible are writ large with expressions of depression and despair: Elijah asked for his life to be taken. Jonah was deeply despondent after God didn't destroy Nineveh as he had prophesied; he sat alone outside the city comforted only by a vine that grew up to shade him from the sun. When the vine withered, Jonah's conclusion was, "It would be better for me to die than to live." Jeremiah lamented the day he had been born. Job's wife advised him to "curse God and die," which could not have been encouraging.

One of the great mysteries of depression is that it seems to be no respecter of persons. People who appear to have everything to live for—career advancement, personal attractiveness, and financial security—are as likely candidates as those on the lowest rungs of the ladder of success. Kings and queens and CEOs join hands with serfs and parking lot attendants in the brotherhood or sisterhood of melancholy. Depression is an equal opportunity employer. No one really has to ask what depression is, because we've all tasted it to one degree or another. Anthony Storr writes, "Depression is part of the experience of every human being" (Storr 1988, 143).

Winston Churchill battled depression. Violet Asquith recorded her first encounter with Churchill, which captures something of both his depression and his strength in combating it. For an hour at dinner he didn't speak, even though she was sitting next to him. His first words were to ask her age, and when she answered he replied with some despair, "I'm thirty-two already." Then defiantly, "Older than anyone else who counts, though." Then savagely, "Curse ruthless time. Curse our mortality. How cruelly short is our allotted span for all we must cram into it. We are worms, all worms. But I do believe I am a glowworm" (Manchester 1983, 367).

Abraham Lincoln suffered bouts of what was then called "melancholy" severe enough to make him consider suicide. During one of his worst bouts he wrote to a friend, "I am now the most miserable man living. If what I feel were equally distributed to the whole human family, there would not be one cheerful face on the earth. Whether I shall ever be better I cannot tell; I awfully forebode I shall not. To remain as I am is impossible; I must die or be better, it appears to me" (Thomas 1952, 72).

John Quincy Adams wrote that when he was a young man he apparently lacked the stuff required to make his way in the world; as an old man he could not look back upon a single episode in his life as a significant achievement and he felt that his existence had been a failure—though he had served with distinction as ambassador, congressman, secretary of state, and U.S. president (Nagel 1983).

Creative people are not exempt. In fact, Anthony Storr argues that writers and artists are more depression-prone than the general population.

Robert Benchley, a humorist and writer who suffered from depression himself, once wrote to Dorothy Parker when she had been hospitalized following one of a number of suicide attempts: "If you don't stop this sort of thing you may seriously damage your health."

Even fictional characters are vulnerable. Sherlock Holmes attempted to self-medicate his bouts of depression with cocaine, at least early in his career.

What exactly is depression? Written attempts to describe it date back at least 4,000 years (Papolos and Papolos 1992). Louis Armstrong is supposed to have said, by way of explaining the blues, "If you have to ask, you'll never know." Depression, the real blues, is probably similar. No single symptom, by itself, can define its presence. Further, it is not always easy to distinguish ordinary, run-of-the-mill unhappiness from clinical depression. In fact, people sometimes report deeper feelings of sadness when depression is *less* serious.

Think of the term *depression* as it is used literally (to depress a lever, for instance). To depress something is to move it from a higher level to a lower level. This movement from high to low captures much of the flavor of psychological depression, which involves a lower amount of energy, lower self-esteem, a lowering of mood, and in general a lowered appetite for life. In fact, ask depressed people how they're feeling and there's a good chance they will respond, "Low."

When you are depressed, you find yourself struggling for energy. Your food seems to lose its flavor, tasks and relationships that used to energize you now feel so draining as not to be worth the effort, and you feel as if you can hardly drag yourself through the day. Tasks as simple as picking up the telephone or writing a letter feel as though they would require superhuman effort. Watching TV is about as far as your ambition goes—if it goes as far as getting out of bed.

You tell yourself to snap out of it. You remind yourself that you have much to be thankful for, that many people in the world are far worse off than you. You resolve that tomorrow you will be back to your old self. But tomorrow comes, and nothing changes. True depression cannot be whisked away by an act of the will.

Although it can be hard to capture in a sentence, depression can generally be effectively diagnosed. In case you haven't experienced it (yet), it typically involves some or all of the following (see Papolos and Papolos 1992):

> depressed mood
> decreased interest in life
> decreased appetite
> suicidal tendencies
> decreased ability to concentrate
> decreased energy
> insomnia or hypersomnia

15

decreased sense of self-worth or well-being

psychomotor retardation

(Of course, an actual diagnosis of depression can only be appropriately made by a licensed professional.)

Depression has a spiral quality to it, as if it were feeding on itself. Many depressed people feel guilty about the fact that they are depressed. This is often true of Christians, who sometimes feel that their depression is an indication of a lack of faith, and that if they simply had as much faith as a "normal" Christian they wouldn't be depressed. Of course such guilt, instead of motivating and empowering change, only serves to make the depressed person that much more depressed.

How bad is it?

Depression affects an estimated 19 million Americans each year, according to the National Institute of Mental Health (NIMH) in 1999 (see NIMH 1999). Dr. Martin Seligman (1990) estimates that at any one time about 25 percent of us are going through an episode of at least mild "normal" depression. It is so prevalent that within mental health circles it is traditionally known as "the common cold of emotional life."

Measured in terms of absenteeism, tardiness, and generally lowered productivity, depression is also expensive. In fact, the NIMH estimated the cost of depression in America in 1999 at more than $30 billion annually.

But the financial cost is small compared to the price paid in human suffering. And the cost in human lives cannot be so readily calculated. An estimated 15 percent of those who suffer from depression take their lives.

Some people are more at risk for depression than others. Historically, depression has been considered more a woman's problem than a man's. Community surveys and treatment programs have estimated that two to six times more women than men are affected by depression. However, a recent study involving 23,000 clients and 500 medical practitioners suggests that may be changing. For one thing, clinicians failed to recognize depression two-thirds of the time it occurred in men (as opposed to one-half the time it occurred in women). Further, men are twice as likely as women to resist visiting a doctor if they are feeling depressed, and doctors are less likely to probe for depression with male clients than with female clients (a study published in *Psychological Assessment*, reported in the *Pasadena Star News*, Dec. 23, 1991).

Despite missed diagnoses in men, depression is still more prevalent in women. This may be partially due to hormonal factors such as postpartum and premenstrual depression. It may also reflect socioeconomic factors like greater financial pressures on women (Dr. Gerald L. Klerman, professor of psychiatry at Cornell University Medical Center, cited in *Pasadena Star News*, Dec. 23, 1991).

Depression tends to be more common in separated or divorced persons than those who are married or who have never married. It also tends to strike people of lower socioeconomic status.

Depression Is on the Rise

Depression seems to be getting worse (which is depressing in itself). People born during the past three decades are three to ten times more likely to become depressed than those born in previous generations. A researcher at the NIMH notes that depression is now striking people in their most productive years, when they are raising young children and attempting to develop their vocational lives (*Los Angeles Times,* Oct. 9, 1988, Part I, 34).

One study asked over 9,000 people if they had ever experienced depressive symptoms. The researchers began with a commonsense assumption that the longer people had lived, the more likely they had experienced depression. They found that people between twenty and twenty-five had a 5 to 6 percent chance of having been depressed, and that those between twenty-five and forty-four were, as they had anticipated, more likely to have been depressed (an 8 to 9 percent chance). However, they were surprised to find that those born before 1925 had only a 4 percent likelihood of ever having been depressed—even though their extra years gave them a larger "window of opportunity," and those born before World War I had only a one percent chance (*Los Angeles Times,* Oct. 9, 1988, Part I, 34).

More recently, Ross (2002, 4) noted that in the United States adult rates of depression and anxiety have tripled since 1990, with at least one in ten children suffering from significant mood disorders. She also pointed out that mood problems are increasing so quickly that by 2020, they will outrank AIDS, violence, and accidents as the major causes of early death and disability.

This raises the question of what might be going on in our culture to make people more vulnerable to depression. Dr. Martin Seligman, a researcher who has done a good deal of studying and writing in this field, is convinced that the rise of depression to epidemic status is related to trends in society as a whole. The loss of a sense of community, the loss of the solidity of the family as the divorce rate has risen, the loss of faith in institutions like government because of political assassinations in the 1960s and Watergate in the 1970s have left people with little to guide them through life other than personal preference. He calls this state of spiritual impoverishment "the California self." (It's not clear why people always pick on California; no one ever rails about the "Idaho" self or the "North Dakota" self, but everyone in California is from some other state anyway.) "Where can one turn now for identity, for satisfaction, and for hope?" Dr. Seligman asked in an address to the American Psychological Association some years ago. "To a very small and frail unit indeed: the self.

"Surely one necessary condition for meaning—assuredly not sufficient—is the attachment to something larger than you are. To the extent that it is now difficult for young people to take seriously their relationship to God, to care about their relationship to the country, or to be part of a large and abiding family, meaning in life will be very difficult to find. The self, to put it another way, is a very poor site for meaning" (Buie 1988, 18).

The church, of course, does not exist primarily as a form of "depression prevention." But it does seem noteworthy that as our society's obsession with individualism moves us farther and farther away from God's call to community and intimacy, we become increasingly vulnerable to problems like depression. Our society's approach to living is not effectively nurturing the human spirit. Later in this book we want to look at how to draw on the church as a healing community

19

(in addition to the other tasks to which it is called) in dealing with depression.

Not only is depression on the rise; some researchers feel that people are becoming depressed at earlier ages than in previous generations. Depression can strike at almost any time in life, including early childhood, although it is most common in adults. One study found that people who were born in the 1930s had their first episode of depression at an average age between thirty and thirty-five, while those born around the mid-1950s had their first episode between twenty and twenty-five (Buie 1988).

According to the Atlanta-based Centers for Disease Control (CDC), the suicide rate for teenagers has quadrupled during the past forty years (*Los Angeles Times,* Nov. 27, 1991, E 2). In one recent twelve-month period, the CDC estimates that 3.6 million students in the United States considered taking their lives, 2.3 million developed a plan for doing so, and about one million actually made an attempt. Of these, 276,000 suffered injuries serious enough to require medical attention.

But statistics aren't the only indicators of the scope of depression in American society. Consider that one of the top-selling books of the past decade is a "how-to" book on suicide called *Final Exit.*

Nor are Christians exempt. Although one will occasionally find churches or religious leaders who argue that firm spiritual commitment should be a safeguard against depression, studies have generally not found significant differences between "religious" and "nonreligious" groups of people in terms of their vulnerability to depression. Psychologist Dr. Archibald Hart estimates that in a typical church at least 5 percent of the congregation will be experiencing significant depression at any given time. Depression, like rain, falls on the just and the unjust alike.

Consider Eva. She had attended church for thirty years; she struggled to maintain the proper image that would reassure others in the church that everything was okay. Each Sunday morning she put on her "church face" before leaving the house. What most people didn't know was that she had been battling depression all those years, that she was marginally functional at work, that she felt utterly without energy and completely defeated in her spiritual life, and kept a bottle of sleeping pills in the medicine cabinet waiting for the day she would have enough courage to take them all.

She could not risk full disclosure to anyone at the church because it would have relegated her to second-string status. She received a general message that depression was the result of a lack of faith, that mature Christians were immune to it, that a truly spiritual person could simply make a "quality choice" not to be depressed, and that depression was evidence of an inferior prayer life. There was no acknowledgment of the complexity of where depression comes from—that, for instance, it might involve a genetic predisposition. So the church, instead of being a place of healing, became a place of hiding.

It might have been some consolation to Eva to learn that great leaders of the faith throughout history have struggled with depression, from theologians like Martin Luther to preachers like Charles Spurgeon. William Cowper, a leading English poet and hymn-writer during the evangelical revival of the eighteenth century, suffered so badly from depression that he spent considerable amounts of time in an asylum, and died—although holding as best he could to the faith—under the belief that he was condemned. Perhaps his best known hymn was, "God moves in a mysterious way his wonders to perform." He wrote those words the night before his second suicide attempt (see Owens 1993).

There is one notable exception to the similarity in frequency of depression between religious and nonreligious populations. Psychiatrist Dr. Janice Egeland has studied depression among the Amish of Lancaster County in Pennsylvania and found that depression without mania occurs only one-fifth to one-tenth as commonly as it does in the rest of the United States. The fact that members of such an isolated subculture experience depression so rarely suggests that cultural trends have contributed greatly to the rise of depression in America.

It is also worth noting that depression, although it is never pleasant, isn't always destructive. Emmy Gut has written that depression is best thought of not as a disease that is to be avoided at all costs but as a process that can be productive or unproductive. What she calls the "basic depressed response" is a kind of turning inward, a withdrawal of energy from the outside world. Depression can be a purposive response, and its purpose is to help the person resolve an inner deadlock that is keeping him or her from functioning effectively; depression is productive when the deadlock is resolved and the person is able to move forward. "I speak of 'productive depression' when at the end of a period of being depressed there is evidence . . . that some useful learning or maturation has occurred, some behavior has been reorganized, some plan revised, so that following the depressed episode we function more effectively

22

in the attainment of some goal, or become more realistic in setting our goal" (Gut 1989, 11–12).

This notion is related to what writers on spiritual life have referred to as the "dark night of the soul," which we'll look at later. The main point to note for now is that depression—although never pleasant—may have an important function to play in human development.

Depression has created vast amounts of misery and suffering for the human race. But there is hope. Research has indicated that over 80 percent of those suffering from depression can be helped with appropriate treatment (Regier et al. 1988). New medications, when appropriately prescribed and carefully monitored, are helping millions of people who would have remained emotionally crippled a few decades ago.

Furthermore, we understand more today than ever before about the causes of depression. There is a powerful link between the way we think and the way we feel and another powerful link between our patterns of behavior and the way we feel. Understanding these links and learning to use them in productive ways have become tremendous weapons in the battle against depression. Helping you discover and employ these weapons is a major focus of this book.

On the other hand, if you feel like you've tried everything else, a movement to combat depression by shopping (known as "retail therapy") has sprung up on the East Coast. A recent poll by the Roper Organization found that shopping was one of the three most highly ranked activities for relieving unpleasant feelings among the population surveyed (*Los Angeles Times,* Nov. 1, 1991, E 7). Not only is it fun, it stimulates the economy, so you can fight psychological and fiscal depression at the same time.

2

Understanding Depression

E motional depression has been described as probably
the most common symptom in the United States
today, and so, as we have seen, it's often called the
common cold of the mind or emotional life (Wright 1988).
A final report by the American Psychological Association's
National Task Force on Women and Depression (McGrath
et al. 1990) noted that depression in all of its varieties or
types is one of the most serious and prevalent mental disorders in this country, afflicting some 20 percent of the
population at some time in their lives, with women being
twice as likely as men to suffer from depression (i.e., major
depression and dysthymia but *not* bipolar or manic-depressive
disorder).

More specifically, major depressive disorder, one main type of clinical depression, is the most frequently diagnosed psychiatric disorder for adults in the United States, with lifetime prevalence rates of 20 to 25 percent for women and 9 to 12 percent for men or point prevalence rates of about 6 percent for women and 3 percent for men (Craighead, Hart et al. 2002). The NIMH recently noted that over 19 million adult Americans will experience some type or form of depression each year. In fact, depression is the leading cause of disability, with annual associated costs totaling over $30 billion. Depression also increases the risk of heart attacks and is a frequent and significant complicating factor in stroke, cancer, and diabetes (NIMH 1999).

Bipolar disorder (previously called manic-depressive disorder), with extreme mood swings or ups and downs and a vulnerability to future episodes, has received increasing attention in recent years. It is estimated that about 1.5 percent of the adult population has classic bipolar disorder, affecting women and men equally, but if subtypes of the disorder are included, the prevalence can be as high as 5 percent (Maj et al. 2002) or even 6.5 percent (Lyles 2001).

Dr. Ellen McGrath (1992) has written a self-help book that shows women how to convert "healthy" depression into new sources of growth and power. The term *depression,* however, can refer to different types of depression and can have a variety of meanings. In order to better help yourself or other people suffering from depression in your church and community, you need to have a better understanding of what depression is really all about. This is important because different types of depression may require different treatments or interventions.

Types of Depression

Depression is not unitary or homogeneous. It is actually heterogeneous and refers to *different* types or kinds of depression with different risk factors involved. Depression does not simply proceed along a continuum from the "blues" to major or severe depression to suicide (McGrath et al. 1990). We need to understand, first of all, the main types or kinds of depression.

It is important to note that *clinical* depression as a psychological or psychiatric disorder is distinct from brief mood fluctuations or so-called normal depressions that we all experience from time to time, those feelings of sadness, disappointment, and frustration that last from fleeting moments or minutes to, at most, a few days. Depression that is diagnosed clinically is a more serious condition that lasts weeks to months, even possibly years.

Before looking at the main types of depression, it may be helpful to review the major symptoms of depression. Dr. Archibald Hart (1987), in his helpful book *Counseling the Depressed*, lists the following symptoms: (1) *mood*—there is an unhappy, sad, "blue," or down mood; (2) *thought*—there is negative and pessimistic thinking, often accompanied by guilt and self-blame, lack of motivation, problems with concentration and even memory, and suicidal thoughts in the more severe depressions; (3) *behavior*—energy is usually low, with retardation, sluggishness, neglect of personal appearance at times, or even agitation; (4) *physical*—several physical symptoms may be present, such as loss of appetite and/or sexual drive, poor or excessive sleep, or loss of weight; (5) *anxiety*—although feeling down or sad is the major emotional char-

27

acteristic of depression, anxiety, fears, tension, uncertainty, and indecisiveness may also be present.

The symptoms just listed apply to depression in its various forms, but in the case of *bipolar* or manic-depressive disorder, periods of depression alternate with periods of mania or mood elevation and excessive energy and behaviors. (If this period is slightly less severe than full-blown mania, it is called hypomania.) Dr. Demitri Papolos and Janice Papolos (1992) have written an excellent reference book for people who suffer from depression and manic depression (i.e., manic depressive or bipolar disorder), and for their families, which they have recently revised and updated again (Papolos and Papolos 1997). They point out that the unipolar form of mood disorder (i.e., depression) is more common than the bipolar, with probably about two-thirds of people suffering from a mood disorder having depression only. However, 10 to 15 percent of those who first experience one or more depressive episodes also have a hypomanic or manic episode later on and are therefore reclassified as having bipolar mood disorder or manic depression.

According to Papolos and Papolos (1992, 8–9), periods of hypomania or the more severe state of mania are characterized by the following symptoms: (1) persistently "high" (euphoric) or irritable (dysphoric) or agitated moods; (2) significant shifts in mood; (3) less need for sleep; (4) disturbances in appetite or eating; (5) increased activity, sociability, or sexual drive; (6) rapid, pressured speech; (7) quickly changing thought patterns that are difficult for others to follow, with racing thoughts; (8) loss of judgment and self-control; (9) impulsive and reckless behavior, especially excessive spending; (10) inflated, grandiose ideas about oneself and one's capabilities; (11) delusional or psychotic thinking, especially of the paranoid type (in the manic state).

The *Diagnostic and Statistical Manual of Mental Disorders* (Fourth Edition) or *DSM-IV* (American Psychiatric Association 1994), or more recently the *DSM-IV-TR* (American Psychiatric Association 2000), identifies five major categories of mood disorders: depressive disorder, bipolar disorders, mood disorders due to a general medical condition, substance-induced mood disorders, and mood disorders not otherwise specified. This book will focus mainly on depressive disorders and, to a lesser extent, on bipolar disorders.

Depression or Depressive Disorder

In order for *major depressive disorder* to be diagnosed, one or more major depressive episodes must have occurred. This means that the depressed person must have experienced at least two weeks of depressed mood (or irritable mood in children or adolescents) or loss of interest or pleasure in almost all activities, together with a minimum of four other symptoms of depression (only three if both depressed mood and loss of interest or pleasure occur) such as: (1) marked weight loss when not dieting, weight gain, or change in appetite; (2) insomnia or excessive sleep; (3) slowed movements or agitation; (4) decreased energy or fatigue; (5) feelings of worthlessness or inappropriate or excessive guilt; (6) indecisiveness or decreased ability to concentrate; and (7) recurrent thoughts of death or suicide. These symptoms (the second to the sixth) must occur almost every day.

29

A milder form of a depressive disorder is *dysthymic disorder.* Here the depressive symptoms are not serious enough to meet the criteria for major depressive disorder, but the person has a depressed mood more days than not for a minimum of two years. The other category of depressive disorder is *depressive disorder not otherwise specified.*

Bipolar Disorder

DSM-IV lists four major types of bipolar disorder: bipolar I disorder, bipolar II disorder (recurrent major depressive episodes with hypomanic episodes), cyclothymic disorder, and bipolar disorder not otherwise specified.

In order for *bipolar I disorder* to be diagnosed there must be: (1) one or more *manic episodes* in which the client feels hyper, extremely "high," wired, or unusually irritable, and gets into trouble, is unable to function at school or work, or ends up being hospitalized; (2) during the *manic episodes,* at least three of the following symptoms present: feeling overly self-confident or even grandiose; needing less sleep than usual; being unable to stop talking; having racing thoughts; being easily distracted; being much more active socially or sexually, or being much more productive at work or at school than usual, or feeling agitated much of the time; getting involved in pleasurable activities without thinking of the consequences (e.g., buying things that are not affordable or having unprotected sex with a stranger); and (3) one or more *depressive episodes* as described earlier for *major depressive disorder.*

In order for *bipolar II disorder* to be diagnosed, there must be: (1) one or more depressive episodes as described for major depressive disorder; and (2) one or more hypomanic episodes that are similar to manic episodes but are not as impairing or severe.

In order for *cyclothymic disorder* to be diagnosed, there must be: (1) mood swings that are unpredictable, with the "ups" less severe than manic episodes and the "downs" less severe than major depressive episodes; (2) reduced productivity and unreliability due to the unstable mood even though it does not cause significant problems per se (Frances and First 1998, 59–78).

Dr. Archibald Hart has pointed out that because depression has many *types,* it is more correct to think of it as a "spectrum" disorder. However, despite its complexity, he notes that it is helpful to view depression as being one or a combination of the following three *things* or *meanings* (see Hart 1987, 43): (1) it can be a *symptom* of something else (e.g., depression can be a side effect of a serious disease or influenza); (2) it can be a *reaction* to life events like bereavement or losing a job, (i.e., *reactive* depression); (3) it can be a *disease* or *disorder* in and of itself (e.g., when the body is suffering from some disorder of the biochemical system that disrupts psychic balance or equilibrium). Dr. Hart has also written a helpful book on how depression can be a healing emotion when you learn how to cooperate with it (Hart 1993).

Causes of Depression

There are a number of possible causes of depression, with various authors emphasizing different causes depending on their theoretical viewpoints and models of depression. The major possible causes of depression include the following.

Physical Factors

Lack of sleep, lack of regular exercise, poor diet or nutrition (see Ross and Roth 1990; Ross 2002), overwork or exhaustion, or some types of physical illness/condition (e.g., hypothyroidism, or an underactive thyroid) can contribute to depression. Postnatal depression, or postbaby blues, is a specific example of how physical or biological factors (associated with childbirth and its aftermath) can lead to depression. Postnatal depression is apparently the most common complication after childbirth and affects about one out of every ten mothers (see Sapsted 1990). Another example of how physical factors like the weather and its effect on our biological systems can make us feel depressed is an acute form of winter depression called seasonal affective disorder, or SAD. It was first identified in the early 1980s, and is characterized by a depressed mood together with overeating, carbohydrate hunger, weight gain, and increased sleep, especially in the morning. SAD affects about 5 to 6 percent of the population, and light is a natural and effective treatment (Rosenthal 1993; Sider 1993). Dr. Peter Whybrow, a psychiatrist, has suggested that underlying SAD symptoms and other feelings of being fat, miserable, and depressed during the dark days of winter (usually October through March in the United States) is the presence of "the hibernation response" in human beings. He describes a number of possible treatments, including phototherapy, or exposure to sufficiently bright lights serving as synthetic sunlight, and an antihibernation diet (see Whybrow and Bahr 1988).

Temperament Vulnerability ("Depression-Prone Personality")

Dr. Frederic Flach has described the depression-prone person with a temperament vulnerability or susceptibility to depression as follows:

The susceptible person is vulnerable to loss . . . if a person has experienced a significant loss during his formative years (e.g., death of a parent), the vulnerability to depression is heightened. The susceptible person is also conscientious, responsible, and has a high personal ethic—quick to feel guilt, whether warranted or not. He may be ambitious, energetic, and competitive in normal spirits. In spite of a tendency to be self-absorbed, he does care about the feelings of others, sometimes too much so, and may be overly cautious lest he inadvertently hurt their feelings. He tends to find himself in deep and sometimes overwhelming involvements, and very dependent on those he loves. He is inflexible—highly sensitive to anything that would decrease his self-esteem in his own eyes or others' eyes. Being rejected is . . . especially painful . . . his need for self-control and control over his environment is strong. He has difficulty managing his hostility—he may not even be aware of his own anger, and finds it difficult to mobilize his emotions in his defense, even when it is justifiable or necessary. (Flach 1974, 41–42)

33

Although this description is somewhat general and does not apply to everyone, it is a helpful reminder that some people are more susceptible or prone to depression, and may therefore need to take special steps to avoid potential depression-producing situations or relationships.

Sin

There are times and occasions when depression may be a consequence of sin in a person's life, but this does *not* mean that all depression is always due to personal sin. Some examples of possible sinful causes of depression include negative, sinful attitudes or feelings like bitterness, resentment, or hatred; guilt and unrepentance over present sinful behavior or attitudes; backsliding or turning away from the Lord and his Word; fear of the future and lack of trust in God as sufficient provider; and unbelief in general.

God-Sent Trials

Difficult, painful, stressful times of trial or struggle may lead to periods of depression. Such God-sent trials are meant, however, to prune or purify us, so that we can bear more fruit (John 15:2; 1 Peter 1:6–7). As someone has put it: "God tries us to bring forth the good in us, whereas Satan tempts us to bring forth the evil or worst in us."

Demonic Attacks

Satan and his demonic forces can attack and oppress people, making them feel depressed and oppressed (see Eph. 6:11–12; 1 Peter 5:8–9).

Loneliness

Loneliness is sometimes defined as the fear of love or the fear of rejection. Such fear or loneliness can result in depression if it leads to withdrawal from much-needed fellowship and interaction with friends and other people.

Triggering Situations

There are a number of situations that can trigger depression or depressive reactions: (a) insult, rejection, or failure; (b) loss—especially of a loved one or object; (c) life stress and change, especially if too much or too quickly (in a short period of time); (d) lack of positive, reinforcing or rewarding events in lifestyle (or loss of the reinforcing or rewarding power of such events); (e) reaction to success (depression can occur *after* a particular experience of success or achievement that may have been very taxing or stressful, and sometimes just *before* such an event); (f) learned helplessness in uncontrollable situations, or learning over a number of experiences that one's responses make no difference to outcomes, leading possibly to passivity and depression (see Seligman 1975, 1990). Seligman's national best-seller (1990) explains how you can change your mind and your life by learned optimism instead of learned helplessness.

Irrational, Unbiblical Self-Talk or Misbeliefs

Cognitive therapists like Dr. Aaron Beck and Dr. Albert Ellis have emphasized that it is really *not* triggering situations (e.g., rejection or failure) per se that result in depression, but a person's *mental attitude* or *self-talk* (implicit beliefs, expectations, interpretations of events/situations, meanings, etc.) in response to such situations that is responsible for emotional states such as depression. Perfectionistic, rigid, absolutistic ways of thinking, often with logical errors (e.g., blowing things out of proportion, or *magnification*; taking things too personally with self-blaming, or *personalization*; focusing only on the negative aspects of a particular situation, or *mental filter/selective abstraction;* jumping to conclusions without adequate evidence, or *arbitrary inference;* etc.) can distort the way one views one's *self,* the *world,* and *the future* in a *negative* direction, often resulting in depression. Dr. William Backus has written a number of helpful books on a Christian approach to cognitive therapy called "misbelief therapy" (e.g., see Backus and Chapian 1980).

Anger Turned Inward against the Self

Some mental health professionals, especially those with a more psychoanalytic or psychodynamic perspective (following Freud and others), suggest that unresolved anger turned inward against one's self can result in depression. Such anger may initially have been directed toward a loved one/object that has been lost. Dr. Gary Collins (1988) has pointed out that hurt may underlie anger and revengefulness, which may eventually result in depression.

Biological Constitutional Factors

Biologically oriented therapists and psychiatrists often attribute severe depression and bipolar (manic depressive) disorders to an imbalance in brain biochemistry that may be related to genetic factors and/or constitutional predispositions, as well as environmental and life stress. More specifically, depression may be due to a deficiency in norepinephrine or serotonin, two well-known neurochemicals needed for proper functioning of brain biochemistry (see Beach, Sandeen, and O'Leary 1990, 27–28). Medical treatments such as antidepressants and/or electroconvulsive shock treatment (ECT or EST) are often recommended for severe depressive disorders. Mood stabilizers or medications such as lithium, depakote (divalproex), and tegretol (carbamazepine) are crucial for treating bipolar disorder. A recent interesting development is the use of omega-3 fatty acids (or fish oils) for bipolar disorder, but more research is needed on this (Stoll 2001). Several mood stabilizers or medications (mainly anticonvulsants) for the treatment of bipolar disorder are also being developed.

Existential Vacuum

Depression may at times be due to meaninglessness and emptiness, or an existential vacuum, in life. Mild depression is experienced by almost every person at times and may be simply due to the "pain of being human" in a fallen world.

Spiritual "Dark Night of the Soul"

There are times when depression is associated with spiritual dryness and an experience that has been called the "dark night of the soul" by St. John of the Cross (cf. Isa.

50:10). Dr. Richard Foster, in his excellent book *Celebration of Discipline,* describes such an experience:

> The "dark night" . . . is not something bad or destructive.
> . . . The purpose of the darkness is not to punish or afflict
> us. It is to set us free . . . What is involved in entering
> the dark night of the soul? It may be a sense of dryness,
> depression, even lostness. It strips us of overdependence
> on the emotional life. The notion, often heard today, that
> such experiences can be avoided and that we should live
> in peace, comfort, joy and celebration only betrays the fact
> that much contemporary experience is surface slush. The
> dark night is one of the ways God brings us to a hush,
> a stillness, so that He can work an inner transformation
> of the soul. . . . Recognize the dark night for what it is.
> Be grateful that God is lovingly drawing you away from
> every distraction so that you can see Him. (Foster 1978,
> 89–91)

Dr. Martyn Lloyd-Jones years ago wrote a helpful book on spiritual depression that can still be read with much benefit (see Lloyd-Jones 1965).

Interpersonal Factors

Serious interpersonal or relationship problems may also lead to depression. For example, about 50 percent of depressed people also experience chronic marital discord, and Beach, Sandeen, and O'Leary (1990) have emphasized that marital discord is both a cause and correlate of depression in a significant number of depressed individuals. They also point out that recent research has shown that marital difficulties and family dysfunction are significant factors affecting the course of depression; high levels of critical communication in the families of depressed individuals in particular have been found to be related to higher relapse rates. Marital therapy for depression has therefore been emphasized as a crucial approach for helping depressed individuals who are married (Beach, Sandeen, and O'Leary 1990). Podell and Shimer (1992) have written a book to help people who are close to a depressed loved one cope better and stay well.

Larger Societal/Cultural Factors

Larger societal and cultural factors like political unrest, economic recession, modernization and industrialization, high divorce rates, and poverty may also contribute to higher rates of depression (see Beach, Sandeen, and O'Leary 1990, 49–51). The actual *expression* of depression in terms of specific symptoms is also affected by ethnic and cultural factors (see Sue and Sue 2003). For example, Asians tend to "somaticize" their depression, showing more somatic or physical symptoms, including loss of appetite, sleep difficulties, and other symptoms like headaches and general aches and pains (see Tan 1989; Tan and Dong 2000).

Psychosocial Treatments for Major Depressive Disorder

Behavior therapy, cognitive-behavior therapy, and *interpersonal psychotherapy* have all been found to be effective psychosocial treatments for major depressive disorder.

Psychosocial and pharmacological or drug interventions for major depressive episodes appear to be equally effective, with some support found for the superior effectiveness of combined psychosocial and pharmacological treatments, although this is less clear for *severely* depressed clients (Craighead, Hart et al. 2002, 245). The following are some helpful books that provide clinical guidelines and methods for the psychosocial treatment of depression: Martell, Addis, and Jacobson (2001) on behavioral activation, an approach to behavior therapy; Beck et al. (1979), Klosko and Sanderson (1999), and Persons, Davidson, and Tompkins (2001) on cognitive therapy or cognitive-behavior therapy; and Klerman et al. (1984), as well as Weissman, Markowitz, and Klerman (2000) on interpersonal therapy.

Causes of Bipolar Disorder

Genetics, biological vulnerabilities, and, to a lesser extent, stress may all be possible causes of bipolar disorder (Miklowitz 2002). The biological vulnerabilities may include disturbances in the production and chemical breakdown (catabolism) of neurotransmitters such as norepinephrine, dopamine, acetylcholine, serotonin, and GABA (gamma-aminobutyric acid), and abnormal production of hormones like cortisol when under stress. While stress does not cause bipolar disorder per se without the crucial roles played by genetics and biological vulnerabilities, stress may increase the likelihood of the occurrence of another episode of mania or depression in someone who already has bipolar disorder. The following types of environmental stress may be particularly significant: major life change (positive or negative), disruptions in sleep-wake cycles, and conflicts with significant others.

Psychosocial Treatments for Bipolar Disorder

Psychosocial treatments for bipolar disorder are *adjunctive* or secondary to the primary treatment involving pharmacological interventions or medications, especially mood stabilizers. Psychosocial treatments have the potential to increase compliance with taking medication, improve quality of life, and enhance strategies for coping with stress. Combining pharmacotherapy and psychosocial treatments for bipolar disorder may therefore significantly lower the risk of relapse and rehospitalization, and improve the quality of life for clients. *Psychoeducation,* involving the provision of information about bipolar disorder and its pharmacological treatment and treatment side effects to clients and their families, has been found to increase compliance with taking medication. *Cognitive-behavior therapy* as an adjunctive treatment is effective in increasing medication adherence, decreasing rehospitalizations, and improving occupational and social functioning. *IPSRT* (a combination of interpersonal psychotherapy, or IPT, and social rhythm therapies, or SRT) has demonstrated its greatest impact on symptoms of depression. Consistency of psychosocial treatments over time may also be a significant factor in the effective helping of bipolar clients. Finally, *marital/family therapy* can be successfully combined with medication to decrease recurrences

41

of bipolar disorder and improve occupational and social functioning (Craighead, Miklowitz, et al. 2002).

The following are helpful books that contain clinical guidelines and methods for the psychosocial treatment of bipolar disorder: Newman et al. (2002), Basco and Rush (1996), and Lam et al. (1999) on cognitive therapy or cognitive-behavior therapy; Weissman, Markowitz, and Klerman (2000) on interpersonal therapy and social rhythm therapies, or IPRST; and Miklowitz and Goldstein (1997) on a family-focused treatment approach (also see Johnson and Leahy 2004).

Many of the strategies for treating depression also apply to bipolar disorder, especially the "downswings" of the disorder. Miklowitz (2002, 153) has provided the following more specific aspects or components of effective psychosocial treatments (i.e., psychoeducation, cognitive-behavior therapy, IPRST, and a family-focused treatment approach) for bipolar disorder, aimed at lowering risk factors and enhancing protective factors for the client:

A. Lowering risk factors such as:
   1. Stressful life changes
   2. Alcohol and drug abuse (and caffeine use)
   3. Sleep deprivation (e.g., staying up all night, jet lag or changing time zones, sudden changes in sleep-wake cycles)
   4. Family distress or other interpersonal conflicts (e.g., high levels of criticism from a spouse or parent, hostile interactions with co-workers or family members)
   5. Inconsistency with medication (e.g., frequently missing one or more dosages, suddenly not taking mood-stabilizing medication)

B. Enhancing protective factors such as:
1. Observing and self-monitoring of client's mood and triggers for mood swings (e.g., by keeping a daily mood chart or social rhythm chart)
2. Maintaining regular daily and nightly routines (e.g., by having a predictable or stable social schedule and going to bed and waking up around the same time each day)
3. Relying on family and social supports (e.g., by clearly communicating with family or relatives and asking for their help in emergencies)
4. Receiving regular medical and psychosocial treatment (e.g., by taking medications regularly, attending support groups, and seeing a psychotherapist or counselor)

Persons with bipolar disorder will usually have psychotherapy or counseling with the following objectives (Miklowitz 2002, 122): to help them make sense of current or past bipolar episodes; to do long-term planning, given their vulnerability to future episodes; to help them accept and adjust to a long-term medication regimen; to identify and develop strategies for effectively coping with stress; to improve their functioning at work or in school; to improve family or marital/romantic relationships; and to help them deal with the stigma of having bipolar disorder.

The possible causes of depression are therefore varied (and not mutually exclusive), just as there are different types of depression that may require different interventions or treatments. Such interventions or treatments for depression have been mentioned only briefly in this chapter, but they will be more fully described in subsequent chapters of this book, which has been written to help you deal more effectively with depression. Before ending the present chapter, there is one more crucial topic we need to consider if we are to understand depression more completely: depression and suicide.

Depression and Suicide

It is well known that individuals with severe depression and bipolar disorder have a high risk for suicide. Dr. Collins (1988, 483) has pointed out that the rise in suicide rates in the past thirty years or so can be described as an "epidemic," with suicide and suicide attempts apparently increasing among children, prisoners, the elderly, young adults, and particularly teenagers (see also Jamison 1999). Christians are also affected. It is important to note the following factors that are associated with a higher risk or potential for suicide (see Kennedy and Charles 1990, 340–41):

1. Age and sex: men, especially those over sixty-five
2. Symptoms: depression, feelings of hopelessness, insomnia or difficulty sleeping, or alcoholism
3. Stress: severe stress
4. Acute versus chronic aspects: sudden or acute onset of particular symptoms means a higher suicide risk
5. Having a suicidal plan: especially if there is a suicidal plan that is lethal, organized, and detailed
6. Lack of resources: no family or friends

7. Prior suicidal behavior: past history of suicidal attempts, especially if many in number
8. Medical status: Presence of chronic, debilitating illness
9. Communication aspects: the person has no outlet or has been rejected by others (This means it is important to take suicide notes seriously.)
10. Reaction of significant others: others punish or reject the person

If you feel that you may be at high risk for suicide, especially if you think frequently of taking your own life and you have a specific plan for doing so, you should consult a mental health professional or your pastor immediately, and talk openly about this as well as other aspects or symptoms of depression described in this chapter that you may be struggling with. Help is available.

Depression is a complex condition to handle or cope with. So is bipolar disorder. However, understanding depression is the first step toward effective coping. The next few chapters will describe in more detail a number of different ways or methods you can use to deal more effectively with depression in your life.

3

Coping with Depression

Know Your ABCs

The way you think can have a profound influence on the way you feel. You greet your boss warmly one morning in the office, but instead of returning your warmth and making small talk, his "hi" is distant and remote. Within a brief period of time, you find yourself feeling down and upset. The morning, which started so brightly, has dulled significantly, and you don't feel much like getting any work done. Later on when you see your boss, you look away and pretend you don't notice him so that you don't have to duplicate an unpleasant experience.

You conclude that the reason you are depressed is because of the way your boss has treated you. However, a whole series of thoughts has been running through your mind since that encounter. If they could be flashed up on a computer terminal, they might look like this:

> My boss must not think highly of my performance at my job.
>
> He really doesn't like me.
>
> He's avoiding me because he's probably going to evaluate me negatively at my next review—I may even lose my job!
>
> This is terrible! I'm failing at this job—I never succeed at anything.

There is, of course, a whole series of other kinds of thoughts that might have occurred to you. These other thoughts would have led to another set of feelings. They might even have been truer than the thoughts you actually had. You might, for instance, have reflected on how your boss usually pays more attention to you, and have concluded that he must be unusually preoccupied with some personal problem. You might have considered how your boss was in a rush to attend a meeting and didn't have time to talk. Or, you might have reflected that your boss is simply not good at making small talk, and that his cursory response was less a statement about you than about his own limited social skills. At an even more philosophical level, you might have concluded that perhaps your boss is not wild about you, but that does not lead inescapably to the conclusion that life is terrible and you are a failure as a human being.

The way you think can greatly influence the way you feel.

There were two brothers, one characterized by unlimited optimism, the other by unlimited pessimism. The parents decided to test their limits; they placed the pessimist in a room filled with the latest treasures from "Toys 'R' Us" and the optimist in a room full of horse manure. After an hour they checked on the boys. The pessimist was miserable and unsatisfied, certain that all the toys would malfunction, lack batteries, or be no fun. The optimist, on the other hand, was smiling from ear to ear and throwing manure all over the room. "What in the world do you have to smile about?" they asked him. "With all this manure, there's got to be a horse around here somewhere," he replied.

The way you think can greatly influence the way you feel.

Some people are bitter that rosebushes have thorns, while others are grateful that thorn bushes have roses.

The way you think can greatly influence the way you feel. But not always. There are times when a person may feel depressed because of biological or other medical reasons, in which case psychiatric or medical help should be sought. Also, some severe depressions or feelings of oppression may involve spiritual issues, including demonization or involvement in the occult, which may call for prayer for deliverance and the mobilization of spiritual resources. Another possibility, as we have already seen, is a "dark night of the soul" experience that God allows for our deepening and growth.

This is an important caveat to keep in mind. It is not always true that we "depress ourselves"; self-blame is not a helpful strategy for coping with depression (in fact, it's often a strategy guaranteed to worsen a depression).

49

However, it is still often true that your thinking influences your feelings. When you feel depressed, you are usually thinking negatively about yourself, your world, and your future.

Go back to the situation with your boss. It seemed as if the *reason* you were depressed was because of the way your boss treated you. You experience this episode as if you and your emotions were simply a victim of your boss's bad behavior.

However, on closer examination it becomes apparent that in between what your boss did to you and your feelings of depression there is another critical component. This critical component is made up of your *interpretation* of what happened—your thoughts, or what is commonly called your "self-talk."

A helpful way of understanding this approach to dealing with depression is what Dr. Albert Ellis, the founder of rational-emotive therapy (RET), or more recently, rational-emotive behavior therapy (REBT), has called the "ABCs" of emotional life (Ellis and Harper 1975).

A stands for activating events or antecedents—the situations that happen to you. In this setting, the antecedent was your boss giving you a response that was short, distant, and cool.

C stands for the consequences, in terms of both feelings and behaviors. Here they would include your feelings of hurt and depression and your avoidance of your boss.

Dr. Ellis maintains that generally people feel as if C is caused by A, that the way they feel is caused by what happened to them. However, in between A and C is B—your beliefs about what it is that has happened to you. In this case the Bs consist of your automatic thoughts—that your boss doesn't like you, that he is going to evaluate your job performance negatively, and so on. So it's not the As that cause the Cs after all. The As trigger specific Bs, or beliefs, which in turn lead to the Cs.

So you see the tremendous power of your beliefs. In many cases they play a crucial role in depression. In general, the beliefs that lead to negative emotional consequences such as depression are often irrational, distorted, and extreme. Such beliefs (or what Dr. William Backus calls "misbeliefs") seem to be convincing at the time they are running through your mind, and often people are barely aware of the presence of such thoughts. That's why they are sometimes called "automatic thoughts." They are something like wearing a wrist watch. After you've worn the watch a while, you're no longer aware of its presence; even though it's still on your wrist, you don't feel it anymore. These thoughts are still in your mind, even though you're hardly aware of them, and they deeply impact the way you feel and live.

The first step in dealing with depression, then, lies in awareness—identifying and recognizing these automatic thoughts. In doing this, it is important to be as specific and concrete as possible. It is not enough simply to say, "I am too tough on myself, and I often have negative thoughts." Such thoughts cannot be effectively dealt with until they are articulated as sharply as possible. It can even be useful to enumerate them and to make the wording of them as precise as you can. Knowing the ABCs of your emotional life is helpful for this purpose.

One way to do this is to keep a diary using the categories of A, B, and C. This will also help you begin to challenge or dispute such thoughts effectively and eventually to replace them with more reasonable, realistic, accurate, and biblical thinking. We'll talk about this more in chapter 6, when we discuss cognitive strategies for dealing with depression.

Now let's look at another set of ABCs. Human experience can be generally divided up into three major dimensions. Here A stands for affect (feelings), B for behavior, and C for cognition (thinking). When you are depressed, you *feel* depressed (that's A), you *behave* in depressed ways (B; for instance, you stay in bed or watch TV most of the day), and you *think* in negative ways (C). Often people think about depression as really only being about feelings—because the feelings associated with depression are frequently so strong. However, depression is also equally about the way you behave and the way you think—no part of life is untouched. This also means that in order to cope effectively with depression, it is important to deal with all three dimensions.

The central task on the affective level is to become aware of your feelings and to do the work of grief and mourning as opposed to running away from it. To talk about "giving yourself permission to grieve" can sound self-indulgent (and of course can be used as an excuse to evade responsible living). However, what we are talking about is the facing of pain that is necessary to grow as a human being. In this context, it is the avoiding of pain and grief that is self-indulgent and unhelpful.

Even the job of becoming aware of your feelings is easier said than done. It is a natural human tendency to run away from unpleasant feelings, so that many of us end up out of touch with the deepest parts of our emotional lives. Even people who are highly intelligent and able to talk about complex ideas fluently may be strangely inarticulate about their emotional experiences. There are others who, because of their cultural or family backgrounds, have not learned to deal with feelings directly and therefore may continue to struggle with being in touch with and expressing their true feelings. Feelings are also difficult because they do not lie under our direct control. Many people try to handle depression by saying to themselves, "*I will not* be sad tomorrow." This is the strategic equivalent of saying to a backseat filled with cranky children, "You kids stop crying and be happy or everybody gets spanked." It is simply a generally ineffective strategy.

The central task in the area of behavior is learning to do constructive and helpful things even when—*especially when*—you don't initially feel like it. It is important to realize that feelings often follow after behavior; you'll often *feel* better after you *do* better. It is very natural for people to think, "I'll do . . . (whatever it is they need to do—make a call, write a note, finish a project) when *I feel* like it." The difficulty is that when you're depressed, you don't feel like it. And your do-nothing-ism becomes another reason to continue being depressed. This is the great catch-22 of depression. It is easier to *behave* yourself into a new way of *feeling* than to *feel* yourself into a new way of *behaving*.

The central task in the area of thinking is probably obvious to you now: identify, challenge, and replace negative, distorted, irrational thinking that is often associated with depression. Most important, you will need to learn to think biblically, or to think in terms of "telling yourself the truth" based on Scripture (see Backus and Chapian 1980). In fact,

St. Paul calls his readers to be transformed and says that this process of transformation takes place by the "renewing" of the mind (Rom. 12:2). This is not just superficial self-talk change, nor is it simply giving assent to certain theological doctrines (though of course this is important); it has to do with a radical metamorphosis in the way one perceives and interprets her or his life and world. Ultimately, this is the work of the Spirit of God, based on the grace and the love God has for us.

In the next three chapters, we will look at these three dimensions—affect, behavior, and cognition—respectively. If you will work diligently—with God's help—at applying this material in your own life, you can make significant strides in your ability to cope with depression.

4

Affect

How Are You Feeling?

S teven was a salesperson in his late thirties. During a
very stressful period at work he found himself putting
in longer hours, getting less rest and exercise, and seeing
less of his family. He also had taken on a few extra projects at
his church, which felt like a drain to him as well. At first he
thought he could get through this highly demanding period
by just "revving his engines," but after a few months he found
himself responding in ways that were unusual for him. He
started sleeping later in the morning—even though now was
the time when he especially needed an early start. He began
to lose motivation in his job, his church, and his family. He
knew his children needed him, but during the hours when
he was home he felt like he simply did not have the energy
to give them much. Sometimes he would wake up in the

middle of the night and stare at the ceiling, wondering what was happening to him. A few times in his office he broke down and wept at his desk, and he wasn't even sure what was triggering his weeping.

"This is ridiculous and weak," he said to himself. "I've just got to snap out of this. I know other people who have given in to their feelings—but that's not me. I just need to pray harder and ask for more strength." But just when he needed prayer the most, Steve found it hardest to pray.

Steve continued to trudge through his days, feeling drained and depressed—but without allowing himself to acknowledge and become more fully aware of what he was really feeling: depression. As a result, he became increasingly isolated and withdrawn, attempting to carry a burden by himself that a lonely human being is ill-equipped to bear.

Many Christians, like Steve, unfortunately, have a tendency to deny, repress, or undervalue feelings. More specifically, they often have a false belief (or misbelief) that it is sinful and unspiritual to experience negative emotions like depression, anxiety, or anger. They therefore have great difficulty acknowledging the presence of these emotions when they do occur.

This is not to say that all emotions are morally neutral. The feelings a person experiences today are to some extent at least the result of choices he or she has made in the past, choices that over time harden into character. The person who consistently chooses to rush is going to experience anger and frustration in a situation where a patient person might experience feelings of mercy. The fall has affected all aspects of human existence—including feelings. Furthermore, feelings are certainly not always reliable guides to actions. They may need to be modified, and the thoughts that often underlie them may also need to be changed.

Nonetheless, it is critically important to acknowledge and explore feelings. This is true for a number of reasons.

First, feelings are a gift from God. The capacity to experience joy, sorrow, anger, and other emotions is a significant part of what it means to be a person created in the image of God. In fact, the Bible itself frequently uses the language of emotions to describe what God experiences himself. For example, it speaks of God being jealous (Exod. 20:5), angry (Deut. 29:27), sorrowful (Gen. 6:5–6), experiencing pleasure (Ps. 149:4), and other emotions. God is described in Scripture as a vividly feeling personal being.

Furthermore, Jesus serves as a model of one who experiences the fullness of emotional life. Jesus was not an emotionless deity of logic and reason alone. In fact, the Gospels describe Jesus as someone who had a wide range of different feelings. The Jesus of the Bible weeps with sadness, smolders with anger, rejoices and mourns, and aches with passionate longing.

Second, feelings often reflect our deepest thoughts. Cognitive therapists refer to such deep thoughts—that have strong feelings attached to them—as "hot cognitions," or what we will call "hot thoughts." For instance, someone asks you how you feel about not receiving a phone call from a good friend for a month. Your initial response is: "It doesn't matter—he's probably busy." However, as you continue talking about this, you start speaking more loudly and rapidly and gesturing more energetically, and you eventually realize that you are feeling some intense or hot emotions like hurt or anger. Upon further reflection, it becomes clear that you have had some deeper hot thoughts, such as "My friend hasn't called me because he doesn't really care about me." Both these hot feelings and hot thoughts are often unpleasant—especially those related to depression—and that is why they have a tendency to lurk out of awareness. By becoming aware of your emotions, it becomes possible to search for the hot thoughts that usually underlie them. Often the heart of change lies in identifying, challenging, and replacing your hot thoughts. We will focus on this process in chapter 6.

Of course, not all hot thoughts need to be modified. Some of them will be helpful, constructive, and biblical, and should be strengthened and reinforced. Being in touch with our feelings may help us gain clarity into those hot thoughts that serve as the bedrock of our lives—our foundational allegiances, loyalties, and values. They become capstone statements, like Nehemiah's "The joy of the LORD is [my] strength" (Neh. 8:10).

Finally, feelings can also serve as a kind of warning system. They may indicate that our biological or physiological system has gone out of whack, and therefore some medical or psychiatric help may be needed. They may also tell us that something is amiss in our relationships with people or with God.

How to Explore Your Feelings

Once you have accepted the importance of becoming aware of your feelings, how do you do it? Here are some suggestions that many people have found helpful.

Exploration of Feelings. You can start by giving yourself permission to experience your feelings and not run away from them. Christians are often reluctant to talk about depression—especially if they are anxious to appear victorious in their spiritual lives. It is very important for you to resist this pressure, so that (at the very least) you can talk to *yourself* about your feelings of depression.

Using a List of Feeling Words. You may have difficulty identifying what feelings you are experiencing. Some people have found it helpful to read through a list of words like the one below, and then check the words that describe their current emotional state.

sad	helpless	useless
angry	exhausted	strong
hurt	moody	bored
happy	guilty	enthusiastic
irritable	ashamed	weak
hopeless	peaceful	unimportant
isolated	worthless	agitated
furious	inadequate	nervous
tired	lonely	fearful
resentful	frustrated	anxious
bitter	confused	contented
sluggish	worn-out	satisfied
depressed	defeated	
thrilled	energetic	

Learning to speak the language of emotions is in many respects like learning to speak any other language. Those who learn to speak a language from infancy tend to be the ones who speak it most fluently. Those who pick up a language as adults often find it to be hard work, requiring much effort and practice. Furthermore, they may never speak the language quite as smoothly or naturally as those who learned it during childhood. You may not have learned how to speak easily about feelings growing up. However, even if you never speak the language of emotions as fluently as some people who have used it all their lives, with effort and practice you can learn to speak it much more effectively than you do today.

Use of an ABC Diary. You may find it helpful to keep a journal in a format that uses the ABCs of emotional life as described by Dr. Albert Ellis and briefly covered in the previous chapter. The "ABC" diary will not only help you be in closer touch with your feelings, but also with your deeper or hot thoughts.

Use of Imagery. Your imagination can be a powerful tool to help you explore your feelings. Here's a method you may find helpful, involving the use of imagery.

Sit in a comfortable chair in a quiet place where you won't be disturbed, and allow yourself to relax as deeply as possible. Take two to three minutes to do this. Then, with both eyes closed, try to imagine as vividly as possible an upsetting scene or event that you have experienced. While replaying or reliving this event in your imagination, try to identify and label whatever feelings may come to the surface.

You may also find it helpful to rate the intensity of such feelings. You can use a scale of 0 to 100, 0 meaning not intense at all, 100 meaning the most intense feeling imaginable.

One cautionary note: This method may best be used with a pastor or trained counselor. The emotions triggered can be so powerful that it's wise to have someone who can guide you through the process.

Self-Disclosure. Self-disclosure involves the opening up to another your deepest thoughts and feelings. This may sound difficult or even unpleasant to you. And, of course, it is not wise to disclose your deepest secrets to casual acquaintances. You need to choose well to whom you open your heart. For people who wrestle with depression, it is often helpful to involve a pastor or trained counselor. These people can provide the kind of attentive listening and empathy or understanding that you will need.

Role-Playing. You may also find it helpful to role-play or act out an interpersonal situation that may be causing some conflict or depression for you. You will need help on this one from a trusted friend, or pastor, or trained counselor.

For example, if you're having conflict with a friend or spouse in which you feel some anger and depression over the other person's harsh and belittling remarks to you, but you're not fully aware of such feelings, role-playing the conflict situation—with you playing yourself and your confidant/confidante playing the other part—may help you get in deeper touch with your feelings in that situation. (Of course, once such feelings are identified, you still must decide how you are going to *act* on them. Identifying the feelings here is not an end in itself.)

How to Cope with Your Feelings

Sometimes depression is biologically based. This is more likely to be true when the depression is severe, or when it involves manic-depressive or bipolar disorder. If depression is a significant struggle for you, you may want to begin by ruling out the possibility of a biologically based depression by consulting a physician or psychiatrist. If your depression *is* biologically based, it is important to have some medical help, because antidepressants or other types of medications can be very effective. It's important to check this out first because if the depression is biologically based it will probably not respond to counseling or self-help efforts without the accompanying help of appropriate medications. If it is bipolar disorder or manic-depressive disorder, then mood stabilizers or medications are crucial in effective treatment.

You may, like many Christians, have serious questions about using powerful medications to alter the way you feel. While we should not resort to medications in a casual or inappropriate way, God has allowed us to make great advances medically to treat problems like depression and bipolar disorder. Such medications, when used appropriately, are not designed to help people escape from reality; in fact, very much the contrary—they help people deal with reality.

Feelings of depression are sometimes associated with loss and grief. This has traditionally been called "reactive depression." Dr. Archibald Hart (1987, 132–45) has described two major categories of losses: concrete or tangible losses (for example, loss of people, cars, pets, money) and abstract losses that do not involve material existence (for instance, loss of status, self-respect, a sense of God's presence). He argues that abstract losses are harder to grieve because we cannot "get our arms around them."

Further, all losses (both concrete and abstract) can be placed into one of three groups: real, imagined, or threatened. Real losses involve losses that have already taken place (for example, the death of a spouse or the loss of a job). Imagined losses are those that exist only in the person's imagination (for instance, a person who thinks her friend no longer likes her when in fact this is not the case). A threatened loss is one that may or may not take place (for instance, a woman has a lump; the biopsy has been performed but the results are not known yet; the woman faces the threatened loss of her health and the possibility of cancer).

Dr. Hart implies that of the three groups, threatened loss is the most difficult to deal with. When a loss is identified as real, the grieving process can start and healing can begin. When a loss is identified as imagined, it is possible for the person to let go of it. However, as long as a loss is merely threatened, it cannot be resolved. The person must move as quickly as possible to identify the loss as either real or imagined. Of course sometimes there is an inevitable waiting period (for instance, a person may have to wait for biopsy results). In such cases it is not possible to rush the conversion of threatened loss into real or imagined loss; here the need is for patience and support.

The following are ten helpful steps for counseling depressed persons who need to deal with losses and work through the grieving process (see Hart 1987, for further details).

1. Identify the losses.
2. Understand every facet of each loss.
3. Separate concrete and abstract losses.
4. Separate imagined, real, and threatened losses.
5. Convert imagined losses into real losses.

6. Convert threatened losses into real losses.
7. Facilitate the grieving process.
8. Face the reality of the loss.
9. Develop a perspective on the loss.
10. Avoid a negative cognitive set (or negative thinking).

A crucial task here is for people who are experiencing reactive depressions to mourn or grieve appropriately, and not to deny their feelings of sadness, depression, or pain. This is especially important from a Christian point of view, since there is a tendency in some circles to have the misbelief that "good Christians should be happy all the time."

Often, underlying feelings of depression is a deep hurt. This may be accompanied by feelings of anger and even resentment. Past events may have left inner wounds that have not yet healed. These events often involve elements of rejection, neglect, deprivation, or abuse. In such situations a specific form of prayer support that might be called "inner healing," or "healing of memories," is often helpful (Flynn and Gregg 1993; Payne 1991; Seamands 1985; Tan 1992, 1996; also see Garzon and Burkett 2002).

The following is a seven-step approach to using inner healing prayer (Tan 1992, 1996).

1. Begin with a prayer for the Lord's guidance and blessing as well as his protection from evil.
2. Use a relaxation strategy to help yourself experience as little anxiety as possible. For example, (1) take some slow, deep breaths; (2) use calming self-talk: "just relax," "take it easy," "let all the tension out"; (3) use

pleasant imagery (for instance, lying on the beach, a beautiful sunset, and so on).

3. Once you feel deeply relaxed, go back in imagination to reenact a past event that has caused deep hurt. Give yourself ample time to have a clear image of the event, as if it is happening all over again, and to feel the intensity of the unpleasant emotions associated with it (for example, hurt, anger, bitterness). This can often bring deep emotion and crying.

4. After allowing sufficient time for step 3 to occur, pray a specific prayer (aloud) asking for the Holy Spirit to minister with his healing power.

5. Now allow the Holy Spirit to minister to you in whatever way is needed. For example, the Holy Spirit might bring to mind a healing image of Jesus' presence, comfort, and love, or may minister in the form of words of Scripture that are helpful or comforting, particular hymns or Christian songs, or even sensations of warmth. Inner healing or healing of memories is therefore not simply "imagery prayer," but it is prayer for God to intervene actively with healing power, and for grace to be made manifest in your life. This can happen in any number of forms, not simply via imagery. Inner healing prayer involves waiting on God; it is not simply a psychological technique.

6. Then close with a brief prayer.

7. Take a few moments to reflect on what happened in prayer. How (if at all) did you sense God speaking to you? There may be a need to repeat this prayer of inner healing numerous times. Also, you may not

experience anything "exceptional" during the prayer, and it is important to remember that this is okay.

This form of prayer is often best experienced with someone else, such as a pastor. Here is an example of what such a session of inner healing prayer might look like.

Mary, a twenty-six-year-old single woman from the congregation, comes to talk with her pastor about feelings of depression. During their interaction, it becomes clear that she felt separated from and rejected by her father, whom she experienced as "just a suit and a briefcase." She also felt distant from her mother, because she came from a large family and felt her mother did not have enough time for her. While her parents did provide for her materially, they failed to give her the love, support, and guidance she felt she needed. Her father was a workaholic who devoted long hours to his job; by the time he came home he was generally tired and fatigued. He had little time or energy to devote to her and consequently had little knowledge of, or interest in, the details of her life.

Mary in particular was haunted by a memory of the time she turned thirteen. Her father didn't get home until she was already in bed, and when she got up to say goodnight, it was clear he had forgotten her birthday. As she reminded him she began to cry, and instead of apologizing he scolded her for "behaving in such an infantile manner" and told her that if she could not conduct herself in a more adult fashion, she didn't deserve to have her birthdays celebrated anyway.

After discussing inner healing prayer together, Mary decided (with the pastor's agreement) that this intervention would be helpful for her. The pastor briefly explained the seven steps, then began by praying, "Dear Lord, thank you for being with us during this time of counseling and inner healing prayer. We ask you to guide us and bless us with the healing power of the Holy Spirit, and protect us from evil. Please come and minister to Mary in a special way with your loving and healing grace. In Jesus' name, Amen."

The pastor next led Mary into a brief time of relaxation exercises. He told her to take a few slow, deep breaths with the following instructions: "Take in a slow, deep breath now, Mary, and fill your lungs to capacity, hold the breath and notice the feelings of tension you're experiencing now. We will count up to 5. 1 . . . 2 . . . 3 . . . 4 . . . 5 [this takes seven to ten seconds]. Now breathe out slowly, and relax. We'll repeat this exercise one more time."

A second technique would be to ask Mary to use some calming self-talk; for example, "Just relax, take it easy, let all your muscles release their tension so that from the top of your head all the way down to your toes you're allowing yourself to feel as relaxed and comfortable as possible." One final technique would be to suggest that Mary imagine a scene that is very pleasant, enjoyable, and relaxing; for instance, lying on the beach, a beautiful sunset, a green meadow, and so on.

Once Mary is feeling quite relaxed, the pastor moves on to the other steps of inner healing prayer as follows.

Pastor: As you're feeling very relaxed now, Mary, I would like you to change the focus of your attention to something that is not as pleasant. In fact, I would like you in your mind's eye to imagine that you are thirteen years old again. Go back and relive that painful event when your father forgot it was your birthday, and you tried to remind him, and he reacted harshly to you. Can you see that happening to you now in your imagination?

Mary: Yes, I'm beginning to see it happening all over again. I can see my father there and hear his harsh and rejecting voice, and I can see myself crying, unable to stop.

Pastor: Good. I would like you to continue to hang on to that scene and the deep feelings that are surfacing right now—don't block them out; experience them as they come. And I would like you to not just look at yourself in that scene, but to *be* yourself in that scene, so that you're feeling those feelings yourself now, in this present moment. I'm going to give you a few moments to let this painful episode unfold.

Mary: . . . this is really painful (she begins to cry).

Pastor: I know this is difficult, but it's important that you not block these feelings. (Pastor pauses a few moments before proceeding.)

Pastor: Mary, can you please tell me now what's going on and what are you experiencing?

Mary: I'm feeling very hurt, and somewhat angry at my father for what he's said to me. It makes me feel like I don't really count to my parents. If I'm honest, it makes me wonder if my father really loves me. I think maybe he doesn't. I feel that I am a nobody, that my life doesn't really matter—I don't think I'm worth loving. I even feel like this as an adult today quite often. That's why I get depressed.

Pastor: I know this must be very painful and difficult for you. I would like to pause here and pray for the

Holy Spirit to come and minister to you in a personal way. "Dear Lord, I ask that you will come by the power of your Holy Spirit to touch and minister your healing love and grace to Mary in this very painful situation, in whatever way is needed or appropriate, according to your will. Thank you, in Jesus' name, Amen."

Pastor (after waiting a few moments): Mary, please tell me what is going on right now—what are you experiencing?

Mary: I am experiencing God's love and comfort. I feel as if Jesus really is with me, and that he is saying to me that he loves me and I am precious to him. It also seems that he is saying that he will never forget my birthday, because he is the one who created me in the first place. I see Jesus holding me gently and telling me that he understands, because he has suffered harsh words from others before as well. I feel a real release from the anger I have for my dad (Mary pauses as she cries gently) . . .

Pastor: Continue to allow the Lord to minister to you in this deep and touching way, Mary . . . (pauses a few moments) Can you tell me again what's happening now?

Mary: I'm feeling much better now, with a deep peace in my heart as I'm experiencing the presence of Jesus with me and his love for me. In fact, I feel that Jesus is gently leading me to the point where I can let go of my resentment and anger against my father, and even forgive him. And I see myself going over to my father and telling him that while it hurt me, I forgive him. In doing this I feel a load lifted off my shoulders.

Pastor: That's wonderful, Mary. Anything else before we close in prayer?

Mary: No. This has just been a very touching experience for me.

Pastor: Okay. Let's close in prayer together. Would you like to start?

Mary: Okay. "Dear Lord, thank you so much for this beautiful time of healing that I've experienced from you. Thank you for your love and your help. Please continue to heal me even more. In Jesus' name, Amen."

Pastor: "Dear Lord, we thank you for your loving, healing power and grace that you've allowed Mary to experience today. Continue your healing work in her life, and please guide us as we go on with the pastoral counseling here. In Jesus' name, Amen." Just before you go, Mary, do you have any comments or questions about this experience you've just had?

Mary: This was a wonderful time for me. Does this mean that although I may have some struggles I won't be depressed anymore?

Pastor: I believe you've had a significant experience of inner healing, but this doesn't necessarily mean you will never be depressed for the rest of your life. Periods of depression are very common, but we can bring such painful times as well as memories before the Lord to receive his help, as we have done today.

It is worth noting that this form of prayer is not a shortcut through the pain of human emotions. Forgiveness takes time, and generally the deeper the hurt the longer the healing. A helpful book in this regard is *Forgive and Forget* by Dr. Lewis Smedes (1984; see also Worthington, 2001, 2003).

In this chapter we've focused on dealing with feelings associated with depression. These feelings are often so powerful that it can be tempting to focus only on feelings. However, in many cases (except perhaps where biological or demonic factors are involved) there are patterns of behavior (as well as of thinking) that are associated with these feelings. So in the following chapter we'll look at strategic behaviors for coping with depression.

5

Behavior

What Are You Doing?

In chapter 3 we saw how the way you think can have a great influence on the way you feel. In this chapter we will look at another profound truth: that what you do—your behavior—can also have a powerful effect on your feelings.

However, if you have ever experienced depression you will have also experienced what might be called the "catch-22" of depression. When you are depressed, you don't feel like doing anything. But when you don't do anything, it makes you feel more depressed.

You can think of the relationship between behavior and feelings in terms of a spiral. In depression this usually involves a downward spiral. The worse you feel, the less you do. And your inactivity causes you to feel guilt and sadness over your passivity, which demotivates you even further—the downward spiral. But the good news is that what goes down can also come up. If you begin to take steps that help you gain a sense of mastery and enjoyment, that help you connect with God and with other people, you will find your feelings begin to change as well. And as your feelings begin to change, you will become increasingly motivated to take positive steps in the future—the upward spiral.

Let's begin by taking a look at what you're doing—or *not* doing—right now. Here are some things that depressed people often find themselves doing: sleeping or just remaining in bed, watching TV, sitting around the house, listening to the radio, crying. You will notice from this list that these kinds of behavior tend to result in further depression, since they are passive, and they allow the depressed person ample opportunity to "marinate" in negative thinking.

On the other hand, there are things that depressed people often find themselves *not* doing, but which they would find helpful if they did: exercising, eating properly, calling a friend, attending a small group meeting, dressing up and going out (rather than staying at home). These kinds of behaviors are relatively active and constructive, and can actually help lift a person's mood.

Therefore, to understand the role behavior plays in depression, you can start by looking at what you're doing right now that is increasing your sense of depression and what you're doing that is combating it. More specifically, you can set some goals for unhelpful behaviors that need to be decreased and for constructive behaviors that you want to increase. It is important that these goals be concrete, practical, and realistic. You want to maximize your odds in successfully meeting your goals.

It is not unusual for depressed people to overwhelm themselves with goals far too large to be realistic, and then when they don't succeed they have one more reason to feel depressed. When you are depressed, a goal that might feel small under other circumstances can seem daunting. This is why it is important for you to break your goals down into very small steps, so that you are more likely to achieve them.

Nevertheless, even with small steps and very achievable goals, your initial reaction may be "I can't do it." Or even more honestly, "I don't *feel* like doing it." At this point it becomes especially important for you to not give in to your feelings but to "just do it," because just doing it usually leads to feeling better. When you're depressed, your first instinct may be "I'll do it when I feel like it." The truth is, you probably won't feel like it *until* you do it. In other words, changing your behavior can have a powerful influence on the way you feel.

Another word about setting goals. It is especially important to pray for wisdom and depend on the Holy Spirit's guidance to discern God's will for your spiritual growth and well-being. Much of the superficiality of present-day writing about depression stems from an approach that views problems as things to be removed as quickly as possible, so that life can be "pain-free and symptom-free." Life is not about the accumulation of pleasure and the avoidance of pain. It is about the transformation, through the power of Jesus Christ, of human beings, who have been distorted by the fall, into the realization of the image of God in which they were originally created. This transformation process will inevitably involve pain, and one form that pain may

75

take is depression. Depression may be not only our enemy, it may sometimes be our teacher. As Dr. Larry Crabb puts it, "Our primary purpose is not to use God to solve problems, but to move through our problems toward finding God" (Crabb 1993, 173).

So the ultimate question to keep in mind is not simply, "Am I making this depression go away?" but "Am I becoming the person God has created me to be in Christ?"

Dealing with Depression

Now let's take a look at a number of things that you can do that many people find helpful in dealing with depression.

Self-Monitoring

How well do you know what you're actually doing throughout the day? Depressed people often have inaccurate perceptions of how they actually spend their time. A helpful way to gain this information is to do what is called "self-monitoring," or attending to specific behaviors that you are involved in during the day. The task of self-monitoring can be divided into three steps.

1. *Record your behavior.* This is usually done in terms of duration (how long), frequency (how often), and intensity. One example of recording your behavior would be to keep a daily activity record. Each night, just before going to bed, write down the primary activities you have been engaged in from waking up until bedtime.

Here's what a daily activity record for a depressed person might look like.

7:00 sleeping
8:00 sleeping
9:00 sleeping
10:00 sleeping
11:00 sleeping
12:00 wake up, watch TV
1:00 watch TV
2:00 eat some lunch
3:00 take a nap
4:00 take a nap, Part II
5:00 wake up, sit around house
6:00 listen to radio, read paper
7:00 eat TV dinner
8:00 sit around the house
9:00 watch TV
10:00 watch TV
11:00 take a long bath, sleep

This daily activity record reflects isolation and inactivity. Once this information is on paper, hour by hour, it is much easier for the depressed person to see the connection between his or her isolation and inactivity and his or her depressed mood.

Self-monitoring can be adapted to help you track an infinite number of behaviors. For example, you might want to track how you are connecting with other people. So you would record how many phone calls you make during the day, and how many face-to-face encounters you have. For some activities, it may be helpful to record the behavior more frequently. For example, you may not be able to remember at the end of the day how many phone calls you have made, so you could write them down at the end of each hour.

2. *Rate your behavior.* A second step in self-monitoring is rating the degree of mastery and pleasure you experience while you are involved in any particular activity (Beck et al. 1979). "Mastery" refers to a sense of accomplishment; "pleasure," to the sense of enjoyment. You can rate these on a 5-point scale, zero being none at all and 5 being the highest level possible. Doing this can help you not only to know what you have done during the day, but also how you experienced each activity. It will become clearer through this process that all activities are not created equal; some will be more likely to be associated with depression, while others will help you more effectively combat depression.

For example, you may rate sleeping 0 on mastery and 1 on pleasure, but reading the newspaper as a 3 on mastery and a 3 on pleasure. If this is the case, then as a "depression-buster" reading the newspaper is a more constructive activity for you than sleeping.

This process of rating your activities may help you to see that at least some activities have given you a sense of pleasure and mastery. One of the damaging effects of depression is that depressed people tend to think in "all-or-nothing" terms and tend to view life as one solid unchanging exercise in being depressed. Rating your activities can help you to gain a more realistic perspective—that your depression does not remain static all day. Your depression fluctuates at least partly as a result of what you are doing. It can help you see that you are not entirely a victim of depression—that your choices do make a difference.

3. *Schedule "strategic behaviors."* The third step of self-monitoring is to schedule more activities that have a high sense of pleasure or mastery (those that consistently bring a rating of 3 or higher) into your daily life. This means that you will use a daily record not just at the end of the day to review, but at the beginning of the day as a planning tool. It may also be helpful to use a daily record, not just on a day-by-day basis, but for a week at a time, so you can schedule most effectively.

It is important not just to plan the activities ahead of time, but also to continue to rate the sense of pleasure and mastery at the end of each day.

Graded Task Assignment

Sometimes when you're depressed, doing even a relatively simple task may feel like moving Mt. Everest. So it is helpful to break a larger task down into smaller and more doable subtasks that you can carry out one at a time (break the mountain down into a series of molehills).

An example of such a graded task assignment could involve paying the bills. Even thinking about going through every outstanding bill and getting each one paid off may be overwhelming to the point of mental paralysis. What may be helpful at this point might be to divide the task into smaller steps: (1) put all the bills in one pile; (2) pay the first two bills, and stop; (3) pay the next two, and continue two at a time until all the bills are paid (assuming this method will pay for bills at a faster rate than bills are coming in!). It is also often helpful to reward yourself after each step in the task has been done. For example, after sorting the bills in the pile, take a fifteen-minute break to listen to a favorite tape. The use of reinforcing self-talk can also be helpful. For instance, say the following: "That's good. I did it! I finished the first step. I can relax and go on to the next step later. Thank you, Lord, that I can receive your power to function in life."

Use of a "Behavioral Experiment"

Depressed people are often perfectionists; they can only tolerate 100 percent success. Even a little failure can feel devastating. If you fall into this category, it can be helpful to try a behavioral experiment that will involve minor but intentional failure.

For instance, you might actually choose to lose a game on purpose in order to experience what it feels like to lose, but in a relatively safe environment, like playing a board game with family members or friends. This may help you to realize that losing a game is not the end of the world, and you don't have to win every time, or be perfect.

Learning to Be Assertive

Some depressed people have difficulty in certain situations because of the inability to assert themselves when appropriate. They may need to learn how to "stand up, speak up, and talk back" when necessary. A helpful book in this regard is *Speak Up! Christian Assertiveness* by Dr. R. K. Sanders and Dr. H. N. Malony (1985).

Assertiveness is an often-misunderstood concept. Many people associate it with aggressiveness or selfishness. Assertiveness actually means saying the right thing, at the right time, in the right way, and from a biblical perspective it also includes not saying anything when God wants us to remain silent. Such Christ-like assertiveness is not only compatible with, but is even necessary for, a life of Christ-like servanthood.

Improving in assertiveness involves not so much acquiring new information as acquiring new skills. That means that simply reading about assertiveness will probably not be enough to help you grow in it greatly. Many people find it helpful to do role playing in situations that require assertiveness—with a pastor, counselor, or trusted friend.

Relaxation/Coping Skills

You may notice yourself becoming tense and anxious in many situations. The following relaxation/coping skills may increase your ability to relax.

a. Slow, deep breathing—take a slow, deep breath, feel the tension rising, then breathe out slowly while you feel the tension being released.
b. Calming self-talk—say things to yourself such as: "Just relax. Take it easy. Allow the tension to unwind. With God's help I can handle this."

c. Pleasant imagery—imagine an enjoyable or pleasant scene, like lying on the beach or taking a walk in the woods.

These techniques can both reduce tension and control negative thinking and feelings. As with assertiveness, these are skills that must be practiced to be acquired. You will find it helpful to practice them once a day and use them in real-life situations whenever you can.

Listening to Music

Soothing, comforting, inspirational music, and singing with praise, being reminded of God's greatness and goodness, can often lift up your spirit and help you to feel less depressed. Of course, worship is not intended to be a means of treating depression, but one of the gifts of authentic worship is its ability to elevate the soul (this theme is often recorded in the Bible; e.g., 1 Sam. 16:23; Pss. 74:21; 147:1).

Taking Care of Your Body

There is often a close connection between the experience of depression and the condition of the body. So taking care of your body can be a helpful way of treating depression. Here are some important aspects:

a. Nutrition—a well-balanced diet with sufficient vitamins and minerals is essential to good mental and physical health. Some writers have begun to emphasize the crucial relationship between nutrition and emotional ups and downs (Ross and Roth 1990; see also Ross 2002).

Ross and Roth (1990) have written about a twenty-one-day mood control diet for conquering depression and fatigue. Omega-3 fatty acids, or fish oils, may have mood-stabilizing properties, but more research is needed (see Stoll 2001).

b. Exercise—committing yourself to a regular exercise program (particularly of the aerobic type like fast walking, jogging, swimming, and so on) can help bring about biochemical changes in your brain that may counteract some of the effects of depression. Such a program doesn't have to be elaborate—thirty minutes a session three times a week will do it (see Hyder 1979; Stamford and Shimer 1990).

c. Sleep—Dr. Archibald Hart has emphasized the need for more sleep for the average person (see Hart 1995). However, the case is a bit complicated for depressed persons. Some of them tend to sleep too much and may actually need to be encouraged to sleep less. This is why you need to get an accurate picture of how much sleep you're actually getting. Although there are individual differences in how much sleep each of us needs, most of us need seven to eight hours of sleep each night. In fact, three big studies, including the most recent one published in the February 2004 issue of the journal *Sleep,* found that people who sleep about seven hours a night live the longest. (*USA Today,* Feb. 9, 2004, 4 D).

Dealing with Seasonal Affective Disorder (SAD)

At least 5 to 6 percent of the population has been affected by SAD to a significant degree (Rosenthal 1993; Sider 1993). If you are one of these individuals, a helpful step would be to get sufficient amounts of light—especially during the winter months when the days are shorter. There are actually special devices, called "light boxes," that help expose people to the right kind of light and the right amount of it. (See Rosenthal 1993, and Whybrow and Bahr 1988, for more information about this problem.)

In this chapter we've focused on behaviors that are connected with depression—what you do can definitely affect how you feel. Now we turn to the next great weapon in battling depression—how you think.

6

Cognition

How Are You Thinking?

As we saw in chapter 3, many people are under the impression that the way they are feeling is a result of the things that happen to them—that pleasant circumstances cause them to feel joy and gratitude, while difficulties cause them to feel sadness and depression. However, more often than not, it is not the things that happen to you that cause you to feel the way you do; it is your *interpretation* of those things. Generally speaking, the way you think can have a great influence over the way you feel.

One of the most significant developments in the field of counseling has been the emergence of cognitive-behavioral approaches to the treatment of depression (e.g., see Beck et al. 1979). Although there are some differences between approaches, a common thread running through them is the view that negative feelings like depression often result from distorted, extreme, irrational, unreasonable, and negative thinking. This insight means that depressed people are not simply victims who must suffer passively from such feelings. They can combat the depression by changing their thinking into more realistic, balanced, positive views of themselves, their world, and their future.

There is also an increasing body of research evidence supporting the effectiveness of these approaches in dealing with depression as well as other emotional problems (Robins and Hayes 1993; see also Chambless and Ollendick 2001; Tan 2001), including Christian approaches to cognitive-behavioral therapy for depression (see Tan and Johnson 2004; Worthington and Sandage 2001).

(As we said earlier, it's important to remember that not all depression is caused by negative thinking. It can involve organic or biological factors or demonization that require appropriate forms of intervention, like medication or prayer for deliverance.)

Authors writing from a Christian point of view (see Tan 1987) have examined the importance of thinking about things like depression from a Christian perspective. One well-known example, called "misbelief therapy," has been developed by Dr. William Backus, who emphasized the need to "tell yourself the truth." (You might want to read *Telling Yourself the Truth,* by William Backus and Marie Chapian [1980].)

The task of thinking involves more than simply learning to think in ways that are less likely to lead to depression. The follower of Christ is invited to be transformed into a new kind of person by the "renewing of [the] mind" (Rom. 12:2). This involves a whole new way of regarding your self, your world, and your future. You are someone who is loved by God, accountable to God, and precious to God. At the same time, Scripture makes it clear that as sinful people we all engage in thinking from a much different vantage point (Rom. 1:21, 28). Therefore, the task of relearning how to think goes beyond simply becoming more rational or realistic in our thought processes. (And, of course, it is a complicated business to decide what rational thinking really is, other than just "the kind of thinking that is most likely to help me achieve my goals in life.") The goal of the follower of Christ is to learn how to think with the mind of Christ (2 Cor. 10:5), to have the same way of thinking that characterized the life of Jesus (Phil. 2:5).

Our goal therefore is not just to learn to think more rationally but also more Christianly. We start by learning to recognize and identify our current patterns of distorted thinking. The reason this step is so vital is that these distorted thoughts become so ingrained in us that we are generally not even aware of the fact that they are there. For this reason they are often called "automatic thoughts."

Patterns of Distorted Thinking

It is important for you to train yourself to begin to notice what now happens without your paying any attention to it. Here are ten common categories of distorted thinking that tend to characterize depressed people. These were first listed in *Feeling Good,* by Dr. David Burns (1980).

All-or-Nothing Thinking

You see things in terms of extremes. If something is not perfect, then it's a total failure; there is no middle ground. An example of this would be: "My sermons are not powerful or effective enough to draw huge crowds to my church. I'm a failure as a preacher and should probably look for some other line of ministry."

Overgeneralization

You take one negative incident and assume it holds true for all times and all places. For example, "I had an argument with my spouse. I have no interpersonal skills at all. I can't get along with anybody."

Mental Filter

This is selective attention, when you focus only on negative details. It is the opposite of wearing rose-colored glasses; instead of making everything look good you make everything look bad. Eeyore from "Winnie the Pooh" is a classic case: wish him happy birthday and he'll respond, "Yes, I'm another year older and closer to death." A more human example would be this kind of thinking: "Oh no, the dessert for the dinner party I'm hosting turned out badly. Nothing else can make up for it; the whole experience is pointless."

Disqualifying the Positive

You discount compliments or positive experiences by manufacturing some reason why they're not really credible.

This allows negative thinking to continue, despite positive evidence to the contrary. For example, "Sure, I got an A on this test, but I was just lucky—he asked questions about material I happened to know. Besides, this is an easy course; if I'd taken a really challenging class, I would have flunked out."

Jumping to Conclusions

You come up with a negative interpretation or conclusion even though it's supported by little or no evidence at all. Dr. Burns divides this into two subcategories:

a. *Mind Reading.* You interpret someone's behavior as reflecting a negative attitude toward you, even though you haven't asked or checked it out to see if it's really true. You have assumed it is true. For example, "Mrs. White looked at her watch while I was talking to her—I must have been very boring to her."

b. *The Fortune-teller Error.* You predict that things will turn out badly, and you are as certain of it as if it were already fact. For example, "No publisher will accept this manuscript for a book; we might as well not even turn it in."

Magnification (Catastrophizing) or Minimization

This involves alternative ways of looking at good and bad news. You exaggerate or magnify the bad and minimize or play down the good. For example, "I yelled at my children. I'm a terrible parent; my kids will need to be in therapy throughout their adult lives" (magnification); or, "I did go to the soup kitchen to help out, but so did everybody else in the church; it's no big deal" (minimization).

Emotional Reasoning

You assume that your negative feelings are an accurate picture of reality. In other words, if you feel "it," then "it" must be true. For instance, "I feel badly about the paper I've just written, therefore it must be a really bad paper."

"Should" Statements

This category, in our opinion, needs some clarification. Some therapists believe all statements that include "should," "must," and "ought" are inappropriately guilt-inducing and should (!) be eliminated entirely. Certainly, many people experience inappropriate guilt because of the pressure they place on themselves. However, some "should" statements reflect ethical demands that may bring about guilt that is both appropriate and potentially helpful (for instance, it would have been a good thing if Adolf Hitler could have experienced guilt for his behavior).

An example of an inappropriate "should" statement would be, "As a good Christian, I should never ever be angry."

Labeling and Mislabeling

This version of overgeneralization involves using names and labels that tend to be negative and extreme. For example, "I didn't pray yesterday. I'm a bad Christian and a terrible sinner."

Personalization

You take responsibility for causing something negative when it wasn't primarily your doing. For example, "The team lost again. It's all my fault."

In addition to these distorted *forms of thinking*, many depressed persons also have distorted beliefs. Dr. Albert Ellis (see Ellis and Harper 1975) has listed some of the most commonly occurring irrational beliefs. Some examples follow.

It is a dire necessity for an adult to be loved or approved by almost everyone for virtually everything he or she does.

One should be thoroughly competent, adequate, and successful in all possible respects.

It is terrible, horrible, and catastrophic when things are not going the way one would like them to go.

While Dr. Ellis has identified a number of such beliefs, some of them are problematic from a biblical point of view. We therefore do not agree with all of his writings. In fact, several authors have written about irrational/unbiblical beliefs or misbeliefs from a Christian perspective.

For example, Dr. Chris Thurman (1989) has provided a list of such beliefs, as well as Scriptures that challenge them. They include the following:

Because I'm a Christian, God will protect me from pain and suffering (see 1 Peter 4:12–13; John 16:33; Phil. 1:29).

It is my Christian duty to meet all the needs of others (see 1 Cor. 12:27–31; Rom. 12:6–7).

A good Christian doesn't feel angry, anxious, or depressed (see John 11:33–35; Mark 14:32–34; Mark 11:15–16; Eph. 4:26).

How to Change Distorted Thinking

Now you have the big picture of how people in general tend to distort their thinking. However, as long as this information remains abstract, it won't be of much help. So we come to the critical step: learning to identify how *you* in particular are prone to distorted thinking. Once you have become aware of those thoughts that tend to lead you toward depression, you can move to the next step of challenging and combating them. Then, when they are lying defeated on your mental battlefield, you can replace them with thoughts that are realistic, truthful, biblical, and accurate.

Here are some ways to help you change distorted thinking.

An "ABC" Diary

We've already looked at the "ABCs" of emotional experience. The first step in changing thinking is to become aware of the negative thoughts underlying the depression. A helpful way of doing this is to keep a daily "ABC" diary. Here's how it works. The diary is divided into three columns, A, B, and C. You should record any event or situation that triggers emotional upset or depressed feelings under column A, and the emotional upset or depressed feelings under column C. Most important, you should write down your thoughts or self-talk associated with the depressed feelings under column B. As far as possible, these should be hot cognitions or hot thoughts associated with deep or gut feelings. These gut feelings recorded under column C should also be rated in terms of their intensity, using a 0 to 100 scale (0 meaning not intense at all; 100 meaning the most intense feeling imaginable). It might look like this.

A	B	C
(Activating event or situation)	(Belief or self-talk)	(Consequences—feelings and behavior)
"I got a C on a test."	"I'm saying to myself that I'm really stupid and dumb. I don't think I'll be able to make it through graduate school. I am a dismal failure and a real disappointment to my family."	"I feel lousy and depressed about this." (depression intensity of 80)

Once you gain skill at becoming aware of the ABCs of your emotional life, two more columns can be added to the diary. Column D stands for "disputations" of the distorted thoughts already recorded in column B. Column E is for the eventual "effects" of the disputations on your feelings and behavior. For example:

D	E
(Disputations)	*(Eventual Effects—feelings and behavior)*
"I don't like getting a C, but it's not the end of the world. I can study harder for the next test and do better. I still have a good chance of making it through graduate school. I'm not really dumb. This C does not make me a failure. And there is no evidence my family is disappointed in me; but even if they were, that wouldn't make me a failure."	"I'm still feeling a bit disappointed with my grade, but I'm no longer depressed or paralyzed over it. In fact, I feel good that I'm able to dispute my thoughts and not be such a victim of my initial feelings." (depression intensity of 20)

The use of an "ABC," and then an "ABCDE" diary can be a very powerful way to help you not only grow aware of but also challenge distorted thinking.

Thought-Stopping

Sometimes you may have trouble controlling recurring thoughts associated with depressed feelings. When this happens, a thought-stopping procedure may be of some help. You should sit back comfortably, with eyes closed, and imagine the negative thoughts recurring. After allowing a few moments for this, you should then shout, "*Stop!*" This may feel awkward the first few times you do it, but it is helpful to actually shout. The *"stop"* shout will usually disrupt your recurrent negative thinking, if only momentarily.

After some practice, you can say *"stop"* quietly, whenever such thoughts occur. Some people find it helpful to wear an elastic band around their wrist and to snap themselves with the band while telling themselves to *"stop"* recurring negative thoughts. Thought-stopping does not always work, but it may stop such recurrent negative thoughts momentarily and help you to switch to more realistic, biblical, and accurate thinking.

Cognitive Restructuring

Cognitive restructuring refers to methods used to change negative, distorted thinking into more realistic, accurate, positive, and biblical thinking (see McMinn 1991; Propst 1988; Wright 1986). The following questions are helpful to ask yourself in the process of cognitive restructuring.

Where is the evidence for your belief or conclusion? (assuming it is a distorted negative belief or conclusion)

What's another way of looking at the situation? (alternative interpretation)

Assuming that your belief or conclusion is correct or true, what then does it mean to you? (the "so what" question)

What do you think God's view of this might be?

A wise use of such questions will help you see that there are alternative, more accurate ways of looking at yourself, your world, and your future that will not lead to depression. You should also strongly dispute the distorted ways of thinking with the more appropriate alternative thoughts.

Dr. Larry Crabb (1977, 1987, 1988) has written some especially helpful material that emphasizes the importance of meeting one's deepest needs for significance (meaning or impact) and security (love or relationship) in a personal, loving relationship with Jesus Christ as Lord and Savior. A fundamental error in thinking, according to Dr. Crabb, is to believe that such needs can be met in the context of achievements, other things, or even other people, apart from an intimate, loving relationship with Jesus Christ.

Prayer with Thanksgiving

The Bible teaches that prayer with thanksgiving can help Christians overcome anxiety (which is often present with depression) and emotional upset (see Phil. 4:6, 7). You may find it helpful to thank God for his blessings in your life, and one of the benefits of this can be a change in your patterns of thinking.

Humor

Proverbs 15:15 and 17:22 speak of the beneficial effects of laughter. Humor can provide a more realistic view of ourselves and the world. Depressed people are generally overserious and often hunger for laughter. Developing a gentle and sensitive sense of humor can be helpful to you.

Self-Help Reading

Although many of the books in the "self-help" section of bookstores may be superficial and banal, there is much thoughtful and helpful material on depression and healthy emotional living in general (e.g., Broida 2001; Burns 1980; Copeland 2001; Greenberger and Padeskey 1995; Lewinsohn et al. 1992; Papolos and Papolos 1997). One of your greatest assets in battling depression is your mind, and it may be highly constructive to think of yourself as a student of healthy emotional living. One way to do this is to keep reading the better books, especially those written from a Christian perspective (e.g., see Biebel and Koenig, 2004; Hart 1993, 2001; Hart and Weber 2002; Minirth and

Meier 1994; Wright 1988). There are also several helpful books on living with bipolar disorder (Fawcett, Golden, and Rosenfeld 2000; Miklowitz 2002; Papolos and Papolos 1999; Scott 2001; Torrey and Knable 2002), including those with a Christian perspective (e.g., see Meier, Arterburn, and Minirth 2001).

Contemplative Prayer and Meditation on Scripture

Prayer and meditation are far more than simple tools to keep us from being depressed; they are essential disciplines for spiritual growth and healthy emotional life. Wise Christians across the centuries have understood the necessity for cultivating and training the mind in order to be able to pray effectively and to allow the Scriptures to transform the way they think. Resources like the *Spiritual Exercises* by Ignatius have helped guide many millions of Christians over hundreds of years. Also, certain passages or texts in the Bible can be especially helpful (see Kruis 2000; Miller 2002) for reflection and meditation by people wrestling with depression (for example, Josh. 1:9; Pss. 23; 42; 43; 51; 62:5–8; 69; Isa. 40:29–31; 41:10; 43:1–4, 25; 44:22; 46:4; 49:15–16; 53:5–6; Hab. 3:17–19; Zeph. 3:17–20; John 14:18, 27; 16:33; Rom. 8:15–39; 1 John 1:9; Rev. 7:16–17).

In these last three chapters, we have looked at steps you can take to change the way you are feeling, behaving, and thinking. However, there are resources available to you that go beyond "self-help." In the next chapter, we will look at what some of these other resources are.

7

Beyond Self-Help

Using Other Resources

I n some areas of life it is easy to know when to look for
help.

Both of the authors of this book have been "diagnosed"
as mechanically dysfunctional when it comes to machinery
of any kind, especially cars. When either of us experiences
car failure on the road, we always do the same thing—check
under the hood. Why we do this is a mystery. There is no
giant "on-off" switch under the hood turned to "off," and
the entire engine isn't missing; in fact, neither of us has the
slightest idea what is wrong or what needs to happen next.
To get the car moving again, we obviously require some
help beyond ourselves.

In people's emotional lives there are times when they
need help beyond themselves. Our emotional lives, like our

cars, get stuck every once in a while. If you have experienced the emotional equivalent of a flat tire—say a mild depression—you may well be able to make whatever repairs are needed on your own (perhaps with some consultation with a good manual). However, there may be times when you find you are stuck, and despite your best efforts, you are unable to get your life moving again. The depression may settle in for the long haul. When this happens, it's time to give serious thought to using resources that go beyond yourself and your own efforts. Let's take a look at when and where to go for further help to get you on the road again.

How to Know When You Need Further Help

Three factors can aid you in determining if you need further help in dealing with your depression:

1. Frequency. This refers to how often you're experiencing depression—daily, weekly, monthly, and so on.
2. Duration. This has to do with the amount of time the depression lasts. It may range from a few hours to weeks or even months.
3. Intensity. This refers to the depth or severity of the depression. It can be rated on a 0 to 100-point scale of depression. This is simply a subjective rating of the level of depression you are feeling emotionally, where 0 equals no depression, 50 equals moderate depression, and 100 equals severe depression.

If you are experiencing depressive episodes quite frequently (daily to several times a week), with a relatively long duration (where the symptoms—although they may be on and off—last over a two-week period or longer), and of significant intensity, then you may want to consider seeking outside help.

You will find that if you have been keeping an "ABC" diary, it will help you in getting a handle on these three dimensions of depression. One of the effects of depression is to alter a person's ability to perceive reality accurately, so having a written record of your daily experience can provide a realistic picture of your depression.

In addition to these three dimensions, it can also be helpful to assess how many of the symptoms of depression—or manic-depression (bipolar disorder)—you are experiencing. (See chapter 2 for a discussion of the most prominent symptoms of both depression and manic-depression or bipolar disorder.) As a general rule, the more of these symptoms you are experiencing—especially if they are persistent—the more seriously you will want to consider seeking outside help. In particular, if you are depressed enough that you often think seriously about taking your own life, you should consult a mental health professional immediately.

Also, aside from symptoms of depression, there may be other reasons why you might want to seek outside help. Depression not only affects people's emotional lives, it also can affect their well-being in a variety of areas, from finances to vocation to relationships, and may result in serious problems, including:

- legal difficulties
- severe financial needs

- need for medical help
- sexual/physical/mental abuse
- substance abuse (it is not uncommon for depressed people to try to "medicate themselves" by using alcohol or drugs in order to numb feelings of depression)
- aggressive behavior
- other emotionally unstable behavior

Where to Go When You Need Further Help

Let's start with some resources that will be needed in cases where depression is particularly severe and persistent. In these cases, seeking the help of a mental health professional is crucial. In cases of severe depression or manic-depression (bipolar disorder), the help of a psychiatrist is particularly important, because appropriate medications, or other medical interventions, may be necessary. Counseling or psychotherapy may also be helpful, and this can be provided by psychologists, psychiatrists, marriage and family therapists, counselors, social workers, psychiatric nurses, or other mental health professionals.

Sometimes, however, a first step is to seek counsel from your own pastor, who may be able to help you decide whether you need to be referred to a mental health professional. Unfortunately, pastors are often thought of (sometimes even by themselves) as sources of cheap, amateur counseling for problems that are not too bad. We believe that, properly understood, pastoral counseling involves attending to the well-being of the total person, with particular attention to the person's connectedness to God. Although most pastors are not mental health professionals, they are often the first "helpers" consulted by depressed parishioners. They can be helpful in providing short-term pastoral care and counseling, as well as in making appropriate referrals.

One specific type of pastoral counseling called "strategic pastoral counseling" has been developed by Dr. David Benner (1992, 2003). It is designed to be brief, time-limited, holistic, structured, spiritually focused, and explicitly Christian, and to involve the parishioner in active study and reading of materials helpful in coping with depression. Pastors using this approach will be active and directive, will develop a counseling relationship that is a collaborative partnership with the parishioner, will concentrate on one central and specific problem, and will maintain the time limitation of the relationship (usually five sessions). (These sessions can be spread over several weeks or even months.) We mention this because, although this book can be used independently, it can also be used in conjunction with strategic pastoral counseling.

In seeking help, it is important that you find a relationship in which you experience a high degree of trust and comfort. Approach the search for a good counselor like a consumer (which in fact you are, if it's a paid relationship). It can be helpful to clarify the goals and expectations of the helping relationship in the first session or two.

Sometimes, finding the right person to help you may require a similarity of fit in ethnic or cultural backgrounds. This is not to say that a counselor must be from the same ethnic or racial group as the counselee, but he or she must be sensitive to the background of the counselee.

One of the problems of depression is that depressed people tend to isolate themselves, and so deprive themselves of caring precisely when they have the greatest need for it. For this reason, involvement in a loving, caring small group of supportive people can be especially important when you are depressed. Even if you feel you are only mildly depressed, small group involvement can be critical not only to keep mild depression from growing deeper, but also to aid you in spiritual and relational growth.

Some churches have also established specialized ministries through small groups like recovery groups (for example, for people struggling with addictions, dysfunctional families, abuse, and so on), and support groups (for instance, for the bereaved, for the unemployed, for single parents, and so on). You may find the emphasis on supportiveness in one of these groups especially helpful.

Many churches have set up lay counseling/caring ministries. The use of lay counselors in the church is a way of expanding the work of pastoral care and counseling. Lay caregivers also usually have more time to give. Seeking the help of a lay counselor may be another option for you. If you decide to seek help from a lay counselor, make sure he or she has been carefully selected and trained, and is continuing to seek regular supervision (see Tan 1991).

Of course, using these resources assumes that you are involved in a church that serves as a healing community. It is important that you choose the right church, one that has a loving, caring environment, giving people permission to acknowledge their problems and struggles and to seek appropriate help and healing (see Crabb 1997, 1999; Ortberg 2003; Tan 2003). However, while the church should be a healing community, that's not all a church is meant to be. The healing dimension of a church must be placed in the context of a community that is also committed to evangelism, world mission, worship, intercessory prayer, spiritual formation and discipleship, leadership training, social action, teaching/preaching ministries, and so forth.

In the context of the healing ministry of the church, many churches have prayer ministry teams that are available to intercede for specific needs of people. You may therefore also find it helpful to ask for such prayer ministry if it's available. Also, your church may have other resources through adult education classes and retreats that focus on growth and healing, parenting and marriage enrichment or relationship enhancement programs, and so forth.

One word about a final resource. Historically, practices that help Christians' spiritual development have been discussed under the category of "spiritual disciplines" (e.g., solitude, prayer, Bible reading and meditation, fasting, worship, fellowship, simplicity, service, witness, etc.). These have sometimes been misunderstood as being restricted to certain "spiritual" activities and have sometimes been pursued under the assumption that if you are "doing lots of disciplines" then your spiritual life is "in order."

It may be helpful to think backwards. Begin by coming to understand what life would look like if you actually lived it the way Jesus taught it to be lived. As you try, you will notice certain obstacles in, say, loving your enemies, or experiencing joy in trials. Here is where spiritual disciplines come in; they are those activities through which you receive power from God to actually live the way Jesus taught. Some of the spiritual disciplines that have been widely practiced (e.g., prayer, Scripture meditation, solitude and silence, fasting, fellowship, worship, service, confession, simplicity, etc.) are discussed in several helpful books (e.g., see Foster 1978, 1988; Ortberg 2002; Tan and Gregg 1997; Tan 2003; Willard 1988). While many of these activities can be practiced alone, others are appropriate only in a corporate setting. This is another reason why being a part of regular fellowship in a Christian church is integral to anyone pursuing spiritual life and wholeness.

You are not alone. We've looked at a number of resources that can help you go beyond self-help in the battle against depression. Of course, these resources are not used in place of, but in conjunction with, all the strategies we discussed earlier that only you—with God's help—can implement. In the final chapter, we examine what one person's struggle with depression might look like.

8

A Case Study

I n this chapter we will look at a hypothetical case study of somebody wrestling with depression. We do this for a couple of reasons. First, you can get a sense of how to apply the material that we have discussed throughout the book. Second, you can also see what might happen if you should decide to seek help through strategic pastoral counseling or another similar short-term structured approach to pastoral counseling. It may be helpful to remember that if you do struggle with depression you are not alone—pastors are asked for help with depression more than any other single problem, except for marital difficulties.

Jim is a single Caucasian male who just recently turned thirty. Although he had been feeling somewhat depressed for a few weeks already, two days before his thirtieth birthday he lost his job, and since then he has been feeling even lower. For the past two weeks since that event, he has had little energy and low motivation, and has been unable to take even normal pleasure in life. Now that he was unemployed, he knew he should be actively searching for work. However, he has found it difficult to motivate himself to put out his résumé and schedule interviews.

Jim had been working as an engineer and had been told by his boss that he was slated for a management position. However, a prolonged downturn in the economy meant that many people had to be laid off, and because of his lack of seniority and age, he was one of them. This was made even more painful to him because of the landmark of turning thirty so quickly afterward. He had thought by then he would be well-established in his field, happily married, and raising a family. But not only was he still single, he had been experiencing increased conflict in his relationship with his girlfriend. They had been dating for the past two years. She was getting impatient with his inability to commit to marriage, but he felt unable to make that commitment, especially given his now-shaky employment status. At the same time, he was afraid of losing her, but he found it difficult to express to her what he was really feeling. He felt like a failure, both vocationally and relationally.

Furthermore, Jim felt his spiritual life was stagnant. He was experiencing "dry spells with God" for some time, just when he felt he needed God most.

Jim knew that he was feeling depressed. He picked up a book on coping with depression to help him try to get a handle on his situation. As he reflected on his experience, he realized he did have some symptoms of depression—a depressed or irritable mood most of the day, a loss of interest and pleasure in most daily activities, and sleeping an unusually large amount of time—though he had even less energy than normal. He also had feelings of worthlessness and of being a failure, and had some difficulties concentrating. However, he was not depressed to the point of contemplating suicide. He was aware that his depression was partly a result of (initially) uncertainty about his job and (ultimately) losing his job.

At first Jim thought that he could handle this problem on his own. The book gave him some ideas for coping with his depression more effectively, and he tried several of them. He attempted to work harder at changing his self-talk, to be more positive and realistic in the way he thought. He tried to include more pleasurable activities during the day. He also started an exercise program, taking brisk walks three times a week, but only kept it up one week. He tried to share some of his struggles with a friend in order to get support and prayer but had trouble opening up to him. Also, his friend didn't seem too understanding. Finally, Jim attempted to explore with his girlfriend the future of their relationship, but he had to admit to her that he simply couldn't get himself to make the commitment she wanted. His girlfriend told him that she was disappointed and upset with him, and that she could not go on like this much longer. This left him feeling more depressed than ever.

At this point, it became clear to Jim that he was stuck, and that to make progress he would need some outside help. He was not sure if he needed professional counseling and decided he would talk with his pastor first. He knew his pastor fairly well; he had been attending the same church since college days. He called his pastor, who assured him that he was glad Jim had taken this step of talking with someone about his difficulties. The pastor set up an appointment with him and told Jim that he usually sees people in pastoral counseling for up to five sessions of about an hour each, spaced out over several weeks. However, if further help were needed, he would make appropriate referrals for Jim or be open to a few more sessions if necessary. Jim was glad to have an appointment set up and looked forward to the first session.

What follows includes discussion that might take place in actual sessions, as well as commentary. In the commentary sections we'll try to look at both how the depression is being addressed in the session, as well as what characteristics to look for in an effective pastoral counselor.

First Session

Jim arrived at the church for his first appointment with the pastor a few minutes late. As the pastor greeted Jim and invited him into his office, Jim apologized for being a little late. They sat down together, and the pastor assured him he was glad Jim had called, and reminded him that they would have about an hour together for this session and that they would probably be meeting a total of five times. The pastor also explained he would keep confidential anything they talked about, except any situations involving danger to self, others, or child or elder abuse.

Then the pastor invited Jim to share more about the concerns he had expressed over the phone.

Jim began by apologizing again for being a bit late but explained he had been having trouble "getting going." He then summarized the concerns described above.

Commentary

During this part of the session, which lasted about fifteen minutes, the pastor said little and mainly listened.

Nonverbally the pastor sought to communicate caring and understanding with a warm and listening posture, which encouraged Jim's openness. Verbally, the few times he spoke were helpful, with appropriate comments like "It must have been very painful to turn thirty after losing your job," and "Sounds like these past two weeks have been really difficult." At this point, a good pastoral counselor will not try to help Jim gain insight or solve problems; instead, his or her primary goal is to communicate empathy and understanding so that Jim can build a relationship of trust. Of course, the pastor himself needs to gain a clear understanding of the nature and severity of Jim's problems. Also, one indication of a good pastoral counselor is that he or she will discuss confidentiality and its limits early on in the first session. It is important when you seek counseling that you understand that confidentiality can and will be broken under certain conditions, such as danger to self (high suicidal risk), danger to others, or child or elder abuse.

At this point the pastor proceeded to ask some questions to get a better picture of Jim's situation.

Pastor: It's quite clear, Jim, that you're feeling depressed: you mentioned feeling down and lacking in energy most of the time, you said you are lying in bed a lot and sleeping more than usual. If I were to ask you to rate the depth of depression on a scale of 0 to 100, 0 meaning no depression, 50 being moderately depressed, and

100 being severely depressed, how would you rate how depressed you are?

Jim: Yes, pastor, I've been feeling depressed a few weeks. I would rate my depression around a 60, although it varies from maybe 40 to 80.

Pastor: Have you ever felt so down that you've had thoughts of ending it all or taking your own life?

Jim: Well, not really. There are times when I've wished that the Lord would take me home.

Pastor: Tell me more of what you mean by that.

Jim: I don't mean that I would kill myself or take my own life, but there are times when I wish I were not alive so that I wouldn't have to face this pain anymore.

Pastor: So you have not had thoughts of actually taking your life, but you've had thoughts of wishing you were in heaven now?

Jim: Yes, that's right.

Pastor: How often do you have these thoughts of wishing you were dead or in heaven?

Jim: Oh, not very often, maybe once every couple of weeks —just fleeting thoughts. By the way, pastor, you don't have to worry about me hurting myself, because as a Christian I believe it's wrong to take your own life, and I wouldn't do that.

Pastor: I appreciate your clarifying that for me, Jim, but it's important for me to ask one more question. Since you don't have thoughts about taking your own life, would it be correct to assume you haven't formed a plan as to how to take your own life?

Jim: Yes, pastor, I have not thought of specific ways of taking my own life.

Pastor: Thank you for your honesty in these areas, Jim. I want you to know it is important for you to contact me if you do at some point have more intense thoughts of wanting to end it all. Jim, I hope you don't mind, but it's important for me to ask one or two more questions so I can get a clear picture of what's going on for you. In addition to your feelings of depression, have you also experienced sudden mood changes in which for a period of time you feel very high, with thoughts racing so quickly that others have a difficult time following you, times in which you speak very quickly and intensely, or when you have difficulty controlling your impulses, for example, going on a spending spree where you spend lots of money?

Jim: You mean like have I ever been hyper and manic, pastor? Unfortunately no, just depressed. I wish I could have that much energy.

Commentary

In this section the pastor does the hard work of exploring the severity and possible type of depression Jim is experiencing. He does this not to play "amateur shrink," but to determine whether a referral to a mental health professional—or even hospitalization—is needed at this time. The pastor asks questions regarding intensity of depression, degree of suicidal risk, and potential presence of a bipolar or manic-depressive disorder. Jim's answers reveal that while he's experiencing moderate depression, it is not severe, suicidal risk is minimal, and a bipolar disorder or manic depression is not indicated. However, the pastor wisely informs Jim to contact him if his depression worsens to the point where more concrete suicidal thoughts and plans emerge. Gauging the severity and type of disorder is especially important in the case of depression.

The next step for the pastor is to explore Jim's central concerns and relevant history before going on to examine Jim's spiritual well-being.

Pastor: Getting back now, Jim, to what we talked about at the beginning of our session, can you tell me more about your family background and how that may have affected the way you're dealing with these issues?

Jim: I was the only child in my family. My parents were pretty normal. I guess it wasn't a "dysfunctional" family or anything. However, I always felt a lot of pressure growing up. It seemed like—especially from my dad—no matter how much I did, it was never enough. If I brought home four As and one B on my report card, he would always ask me to explain why I'd slipped to a B. I would promise to try harder the next term, and I would, but he was never satisfied, and I guess I've learned never to be satisfied myself. Another thing that was hard for me was that my dad was really into athletics. Sports were okay, but I never did that well at them. My first year in high school I went out for football—my dad had been a good football player in high school and college and was always after me to follow in his steps—and I got cut from the team the last day of practice. When my dad found out, he started to yell at me and to ask why I hadn't tried harder. I started to cry, and he looked at me with such disgust in his eyes. I remember him saying to my mom, "Well, you always wanted a daughter. I guess you got your wish." This memory has stayed with me over the years and continues to haunt me from time to time. I guess because of these experiences I've always been hard on myself and prone to feelings of depression from time to time.

Pastor: It sounds like your parents, especially your dad, have had very high and even perfectionistic standards for you in both sports and academics. You felt over the years that you've never been quite good enough; in fact, some of your memories remain with you to this day. You have become hard on yourself. It must be difficult and painful for you to carry such a burden for so long in your life.

Jim: It has been very hard—it's nice to know you understand. I've tried to share this with a few of my friends, but they just tell me I should leave the past behind and trust God more.

Pastor: Tell me more about your spiritual life and your experience of God.

Jim: I became a Christian in college, and I found in God a love I never found at home. But more recently my spiritual life feels dry. I've tried to pray more and read the Bible more, but nothing seems to come of it. Lately, to tell the truth, I haven't even felt like praying at all. Maybe my problem is I'm not having enough faith in God. Sometimes I think God is really angry at me—not only am I a failure in my work and relationships, I feel like a spiritual failure as well.

Pastor: I can see you are feeling discouraged and empty in your spiritual life; I'm not sure, though, that God is angry at you in the way you feel he is. When you think of God, what usually comes to your mind?

Jim: Well, I know God is my father, I know he loves me, and I have felt his love in the past, but I guess lately I have not experienced God much as a loving father— more as a taskmaster that I keep failing. That's why I've thought more of how angry he is with me at this time.

115

Pastor: It is common for depressed people to have negative thoughts about themselves, their world, and their experience with God. Often these thoughts contain some distortions. I think it will be helpful for us to have a closer look at them in coming sessions.

Commentary

The pastor asked Jim about his family background and how it related to his present struggles, because negative thinking and perfectionistic, harsh self-evaluations associated with depression may have their roots in earlier family relationships, especially between parents and children. In an effective counseling relationship, relevant issues of family and personal history will be explored in constructive ways. Here, for instance, the pastor helped Jim discuss not only how his father had imposed perfectionistic and harsh standards of performance on him, but he also helped Jim face up to a traumatic memory connected with an athletic failure that has continued to affect Jim.

In pastoral counseling, you will not only want to look at psychological symptoms but also examine the spiritual meaning of your situation. The pastor therefore went on to explore Jim's spiritual life and experience of God. Again, it was obvious that Jim has some serious blocks and distortions in his perception of God as an angry God, and not as loving as he once experienced him. This is another area that will require further intervention from the pastor in the sessions to come. The pastor pointed this out briefly, but throughout the session maintained a basically empathic,

116

warm, caring stance to listen: he did not give premature advice, and this was appreciated by Jim.

The last ten or fifteen minutes of this session were devoted to pulling this material together and arriving at a mutually agreeable focus (and goals) for counseling, which is the final task of the first session. If you seek counseling, it may well be worth spending some time before the initial session thinking about what goals you would like to accomplish through counseling.

> *Pastor:* In our last few minutes, let me try to summarize what we've been over today. Let me begin by saying how much I appreciate your openness. We haven't had enough time to cover every concern in detail—for instance, your relationship with your girlfriend—but it sounds like these are your major concerns: your feelings of depression and fatigue, your loss of a job and feelings of failure and worry about the future, conflict in your relationship with your girlfriend, dryness in your spiritual life, memories of your dad being especially harsh with you—in particular when you didn't make the football team. Is this on the right track?
>
> *Jim:* Yes, that captures it. Thanks for really listening to me today; I feel a little better already.
>
> *Pastor:* Jim, it's important for you to tell me, out of these things you've brought up today, which are the ones you really want to focus on, and what goals would you like to work on?
>
> *Jim:* Well, I'd like to overcome my feelings of depression and be able to find a job soon. I would also like to straighten out my relationship with God so I can experience him as a loving father. I guess I might need to

117

deal with some of my past pain about my dad and how he treated me. Finally, if we have enough time, I'd like to discuss my relationship with my girlfriend.

Pastor: As I mentioned earlier, often I've found with people that the way they think about things has a big impact on how they feel and what they do. A depressed person often finds his or her thinking has been distorted in negative ways. I'd like to help you become more aware of such ways of thinking and how they can be changed for the better in our coming sessions. To help us with this, I'd like to recommend as homework for you a book by William Backus and Marie Chapian entitled *Telling Yourself the Truth.* It is a Christian book to help us change our thinking. Here's a copy you can borrow from me till our next session. Do you feel up to reading at least a few chapters before we meet again next week?

Jim: I used to love reading. I have a harder time now, but I would like to read it.

Pastor: Let me suggest in the four sessions we have left that we meet again next week; then the last three sessions we have we will space out once every three weeks or so. How does that sound?

Jim: Sounds fine to me. I hope I'm not imposing too much on your time; I really appreciate this.

Pastor: No problem at all, Jim, this is why I'm here. By the way, as we end, how would you feel if we closed in prayer together?

Jim: I would like that very much.

The pastor and Jim close in prayer and set an appointment for the next week.

Commentary

You may find it helpful, at the close of each session, to summarize the main issues that were covered during your time together. You may also want to review any homework that you may be doing in between sessions.

We have gone into considerable detail to get a thorough picture of what might go on in a session. Now we'll look at some more sessions a bit more briefly.

Second Session

In the second session, the pastor began by asking Jim how his week had gone since they met. Jim responded that he had begun to feel better. He had read most of the book the pastor had assigned and found it helpful. The pastor then asked Jim what parts of the book he found particularly helpful and how he had applied them. Jim replied that the book had helped him to see how his extreme negative thinking or misbeliefs contributed to his feelings of depression. He had even begun to identify some of the specific misbeliefs he had, as well as to challenge them; and following the book's suggestions, he had tried to allow the Bible to guide him in the process.

The pastor then asked for some specific examples of misbeliefs Jim had identified.

Jim: Well, pastor, I realized this week one time when I was still feeling down about losing my job that I was saying things to myself like "I must not be very good at my job. If I were good, I wouldn't have been laid off. They only lay off marginal workers. I'll never have a successful career now. I don't think I can find another job, so what's the use of trying?" I guess I do say quite a few negative things about myself—I hadn't realized how much of that was going on. The book has helped me not only to identify such negative thoughts but also to challenge them when they are not true. I've begun to tell myself the truth, by reminding myself that the company actually has laid off some people who I know are very competent—some top management types. So I know—when I think about it more carefully—that the fact that I got laid off does not necessarily mean I'm incompetent.

Pastor: I'm glad you are beginning to see how negative thinking can lead to negative feelings, and that you've used the book to challenge your misbeliefs. Since you've started to tell yourself the truth—like in this instance—how do you find yourself feeling when you dispute the negative thinking?

Jim: Well, . . . to tell you the truth, pastor, it does help me to feel a little bit better but not a great deal better. Although I know in my head that being laid off does not mean I'm no good, I have to be honest with you—I still feel that I'm not that good. I guess it's hard to fully feel or believe the truth. The misbeliefs still seem to be so powerful. Sometimes disputing them just feels like playing a game or some kind of psychological trick. It doesn't feel real.

Pastor: I'm glad you're being so honest with me. I want to reassure you that at the early stages of trying to challenge our misbeliefs, many of us feel exactly what you've described. Telling yourself the truth doesn't feel absolutely convincing yet. It's important to remember that learning to tell yourself the truth is like any other learned skill—it takes time and practice before it feels natural. It's much like learning to ride a bike and drive a car. At first it feels awkward and makes you self-conscious. But eventually—if you stick with it—it will become second nature.

Commentary

Many people find it helpful to do homework assignments in between sessions as a way of "extending the session" into their regular life. It is important to review how the homework went when you meet during the next session.

After more discussion of Jim's misbeliefs, the pastor moved toward talking about further homework—asking Jim to maintain an "ABC" diary to keep track of his thoughts and feelings, as well as to challenge or dispute his misbeliefs. They went through an example of how to use such a diary.

If homework is a part of the counseling process, you'll want to make sure you're clear about what your part is. Effective counselors often walk through exercises like an "ABC" diary so you get a feel for how it works most effectively.

For a large part of the remainder of the session the pastor explored Jim's thoughts and feelings about God. He discovered that Jim would like to know more about the love of God in his heart as well as his head. Jim hasn't experienced God's love very much. The pastor also helped Jim challenge a few misbeliefs about how God is feeling about him—that God doesn't care about him anymore, that he is a failure in God's eyes. After some discussion based on the teachings of Scripture, Jim was able to conclude that God will always love him as his child no matter what happens in his career. Jim seemed to have caught a deeper sense of God's grace. However, Jim did express a continuing difficulty relating to God as loving Father in his prayer life because images of his relationship with his own father got in the way. They agreed that further work on this image of God as a demanding, never satisfied, unloving father would be needed in future sessions.

They set a date for their next session in three weeks, mainly because Jim felt he was doing well enough to wait that long and had some homework to help him along, including reading a book entitled *Love Beyond Reason: Moving God's Love from Your Head to Your Heart* (Ortberg 1998). They then closed in prayer.

Third Session

After three weeks Jim came into the third session and told the pastor he had both good news and bad news. The good news was that he had been feeling significantly better for the first two weeks after the last session. He had been using the "ABC" diary, and he was feeling less depressed and for the first time in a while was feeling hopeful. He was even starting to feel that God did love him. But the bad news was that he had experienced a significant setback. A former colleague at work, who had also recently been laid off, had received two job offers in the space of a week and had chosen one that actually paid him more than his old job. Jim told the pastor that this phone call triggered a series of negative thoughts about him being incompetent, about the future being hopeless, about other friends finding jobs while he probably would never be able to find one. He also acknowledged that he was again feeling quite depressed (though with no suicidal thoughts or plans). The pastor began to explore Jim's thoughts and feelings more deeply and to do more cognitive restructuring of Jim's negative self-talk as well as his underlying basic assumptions.

Pastor: I'm sorry to hear you've had a setback, although it sounds like things went well the first two weeks. Let's take some time to explore your thoughts and feelings a bit more deeply. But before we do that, I want to reassure you that it is not uncommon for people to have ups and downs and to have setbacks like you've had. Let's go back to exploring your thoughts about being incompetent—what's the evidence?

Jim: This is what really bothers me. To be honest, I did have a few reports from a supervisor that were below average. What was really painful was that I applied for the same job that my colleague did, and he beat me out. That seals it.

Pastor: Okay, Jim. You know you tend to focus on evidence that might support your negative conclusion that you're incompetent. But let us suppose that you *really are* incompetent in some of the areas of your former job. So what does this mean to you?

Jim: So you're saying, "So what" if I'm incompetent? It would feel like the end of the world. I don't think I could live with that. I've been doing all this work to convince myself that I am competent, and now you want me to consider the possibility that I'm not?

Pastor: Jim, you know I do not believe that you are incompetent. But we need to get to the bottom-line, basic assumptions that govern the way you think. It sounds to me, Jim, like you have a basic assumption that you must be competent in order for life to be worth living. In other words, if you're incompetent, it's terrible, it's intolerable, it's the end of the world.

Jim: I guess you've put your finger on the core of how I think and feel deep inside.

Pastor: Here's another way of looking at it. Although it might be painful and inconvenient to be incompetent in some areas, it is *not* terrible, intolerable, or the end of the world. Everybody is incompetent in some areas. Besides, competency is not the basis of our worth as persons or what makes life worth living. We need to come back again, Jim, to the fact that God loves us, and his grace is sufficient for life. He accepts us as we are.

Jim: Well, I guess I see your point, but it's going to take a while to sink in. I suppose it's not the end of the world if I am incompetent in some things. I suppose it wouldn't be fair to say paralyzed people or mentally disabled people don't deserve to live just because they're incompetent in some areas. Again, pastor, I've experienced something of God's love and grace. But I still feel some kind of a block—I think it has something to do with my dad.

Pastor: Thank you for expressing that, Jim. There is a procedure called inner healing prayer, which can help in the healing of memories, that may be helpful for us to engage in during our next session. Let me explain the steps of this kind of prayer for you briefly. Also, I would like you to read a book by David Seamands called *Healing of Memories*.

Commentary

Setbacks are not uncommon for depressed persons, who need assurance that having a setback does not mean they are failing. However, setbacks need to be explored more deeply because there usually are other underlying assumptions that must be elicited, identified, and eventually challenged. Here the pastor helped Jim to see that beneath his thinking about competency was a basic assumption that if he were not competent, life would not be worth living. In other words, that competency was his fundamental grounds for worth. The pastor helped Jim to see this by asking the "So what" question but phrasing it in a gentle way ("So what does it mean to you . . .").

The pastor also pointed Jim to God's love and grace as the ultimate foundation of self-worth and meaning in life, rather than other criteria like competency. God's grace and love are often not experienced deeply by depressed persons, and the need for interventions such as inner healing prayer is often indicated. In Jim's case it became obvious that he had a block from the past that could benefit from inner healing prayer, leading to the pastor's proposal for a future time of prayer as well as a reading assignment.

Jim responded positively to this suggestion and agreed to read the book. They decided to meet again in three weeks for the fourth session.

Before the pastor and Jim closed in prayer, the pastor took the last few minutes to touch base with Jim on the other areas of his life. He reminded Jim of some behavioral steps that could be helpful in coping with his depression: exercising three times a week, continuing to attend church gatherings, trying to get up at a regular hour each day, continuing to apply for jobs, and calling a couple of close friends for support. He encouraged Jim to continue times of prayer. The pastor also reminded Jim that they had two sessions left before they would be finished.

Fourth Session

Jim came in and updated the pastor on how the last three weeks had gone. Jim had been walking three or four times a week and said that as he felt better physically he also felt better emotionally. This made it easier for him to keep getting up in the morning at a regular time. He also continued to apply for work. Although it was painful to apply and not get the job, it did give him an opportunity to continue to work at disputing thoughts about his old assumption that career competency was the only thing that made life worth living. He called a couple of close friends one day when he was feeling especially down and reported that making the calls was helpful, both because his friends were supportive and because it felt good to take an active step and not simply sit around waiting for the depressed feeling to go away. He said that he had continued to attend church, but that it didn't feel too helpful because God felt distant and uncaring. The pastor asked him how he had found the book *Healing of Memories*.

> *Jim:* I have read Seamand's book and found it beneficial and interesting. I do feel that inner healing prayer would be something helpful in my situation. Could we try it today?

Pastor: Yes, I was prepared to try it today, as we had discussed last time, as long as you are willing and feel ready for it. As you know, this may take some time, so why don't we start at this point by focusing on a particular memory involving your dad that we can use in our inner healing prayer. What specific memory would you like to focus on?

Jim: The one that comes to mind was when I was cut from the football team, and my dad yelled at me and I started to cry.

Pastor: I remember that. Let's begin the inner healing prayer time now. I'll open with prayer.

Commentary

The pastor began by reviewing with Jim what had happened since their last session. He noted Jim's progress, as well as checking again on homework. The behavioral strategies for coping with depression can play a major role—getting regular exercise, getting in touch with friends, and so on. Jim's continual struggles in his relationship with God, his experiencing God as distant from him, provided a natural bridge to the inner healing prayer time they had discussed in the previous session. In response to the pastor's request, Jim provided a specific memory in the past for them to use in the inner healing prayer time. The pastor then took Jim through the seven steps of inner healing prayer described in an earlier chapter: opening prayer for guidance, healing, and protection; relaxation; use of guided imagery or visualization to relive the painful traumatic experience; prayer for the Holy Spirit's healing and ministry; asking Jim what he

127

was experiencing and feeling; closing prayer by the pastor and Jim; and finally, a time of debriefing and discussion before ending the session.

For Jim, inner healing prayer was a powerful step. After closing in prayer, the pastor debriefed the experience with Jim, who felt more confident now that his relationship with God could become more intimate. He agreed to incorporate inner healing prayer into his personal prayer life.

Before ending the session, the pastor explored with Jim one other topic Jim wanted to discuss: his relationship with his girlfriend. Jim decided he would call his girlfriend before his final session with the pastor and talk with her further about their relationship, even though she had said she wanted to break up. Jim realized he was more open to making a commitment to his girlfriend than he thought. It was now clear that one hindrance to a commitment had been his feelings of incompetence and inadequacy related to his job.

They scheduled their next session in a month's time, and the pastor reminded Jim that the next session would be their last. He asked Jim how he felt about ending soon. Jim said the sessions so far had been helpful to him, and while he was a little sad they would end soon, he felt confident enough that he could make further progress on his own, with some support from friends.

The pastor and Jim also decided that Jim did not need referral for professional help. However, the pastor did make one "referral": he encouraged Jim to join a small group in the church. This would help Jim develop deeper relationships and would assist him in his spiritual growth and his ability to receive love from God. Jim responded positively to this referral.

128

Fifth Session

Four weeks later Jim came in for his final session in clearly better spirits. He smiled more and expressed appreciation to the pastor for the help he had received so far. He told the pastor he'd been feeling less depressed and more energetic this last month. He had continued to exercise or walk on a regular basis and had kept in touch with his close friends. He also attended a small group in church for the first time and said he thought it would be helpful. He even met with his girlfriend on two occasions to talk about their relationship further. They decided not to break off, because he was more open now to making a commitment to marriage. He had applied for several jobs, and while he still had not received any job offers, he was scheduled for several interviews over the next two weeks. He felt good about this but noted that his career or work was no longer the basis of his self-worth.

He also had experienced greater intimacy with God in his times of prayer. He had been using the inner healing prayer strategy with significant benefit. Overall, he was now feeling more hopeful about the future and noted that his faith in God had grown some. He was also ready to work on forgiving his parents, having realized that forgiveness and reconciliation were important parts of the healing process. The pastor recommended two books by Lewis Smedes for Jim's personal reading: *Forgive and Forget* (Smedes 1984) and *Shame and Grace* (Smedes 1993).

At this point, the pastor and Jim spent a significant amount of time summarizing their work. After they had done this, there was one final remaining issue Jim wanted to mention briefly.

Jim: The one other issue has to do with my girlfriend. Although we didn't talk about this one as much, I do feel more ready now to face the issue of commitment. At least I'm talking about it with her, so I feel ready to face this one. I am realizing I don't want to lose her.

Pastor: Are there any remaining concerns you want to bring up before we end?

Jim: Not really. Except to thank you for your help. It's made a big difference.

Pastor: It's been a pleasure working with you. I hope you'll continue to use the tools we've worked on—I'm sure life will still have ups and downs! Although we're ending today, I want you to know if there's ever a need for you to contact me again, you can feel free to do so. Also, from time to time when I see you at church I'll check in and ask you how you're doing—not in public, I won't embarrass you!—if it's okay with you.

Jim: That would be good; I'd like that.

Pastor: Let's finish by praying together.

Commentary

The pastor and Jim began by reviewing what had happened over the course of pastoral counseling. A referral was made to a small group in the previous session, and the pastor followed up on this by encouraging Jim to continue to attend. In doing this the pastor wisely brought in the resources of the church to help Jim. He did not make the mistake of compartmentalizing pastoral counseling by separating it from the rest of the life of the church as a healing community. Although the sessions between Jim and his pastor have ended, their relationship as pastor and parishioner, of course, continues.

Although no one's struggle with depression will look exactly like Jim's (depressions, like snowflakes, are always unique), the principles and strategies for coping with depression that we have laid out in this chapter can be helpful to almost anybody struggling with depression. Begin by applying them to yourself, but remember you are not alone. If there is a need, don't hesitate to seek the help of your pastor or of a mental health professional. Above all, remember that God is with you, and that the deepest depression cannot put you beyond the reach of his love (see Ortberg 1998, 2001; see also Crabb 2001, 2002; Tan 2003).

References

American Psychiatric Association. 1994. *Diagnostic and Statistical Manual of Mental Disorders*. 4th ed. Washington, D.C.: American Psychiatric Association.

———. 2000. *Diagnostic and Statistical Manual of Mental Disorders*. 4th ed., text revision. Washington, D.C.: American Psychiatric Association.

Backus, W., and M. Chapian. 1980. *Telling Yourself the Truth*. Minneapolis: Bethany House.

Basco, M. R., and A. J. Rush. 1996. *Cognitive-Behavioral Therapy for Bipolar Disorder*. New York: Guilford.

Beach, S. R. H., E. E. Sandeen, and K. D. O'Leary. 1990. *Depression in Marriage: A Model for Etiology and Treatment*. New York: Guilford.

Beck, A. T., A. J. Rush, B. F. Shaw, and G. Emery. 1979. *Cognitive Therapy of Depression*. New York: Guilford.

Benner, D. 1992. *Strategic Pastoral Counseling*. Grand Rapids: Baker.

———. 2003. *Strategic Pastoral Counseling*. 2nd ed. Grand Rapids: Baker.

133

Biebel, D. B., and H. G. Koenig. 2004. *New Light on Depression*. Grand Rapids: Zondervan.

Broida, M. 2001. *New Hope for People with Depression*. Roseville, Calif.: Prima.

Buie, J. 1988. "Me" decades generate depression. *American Psychological Association Monitor* (October): 18.

Burns, D. 1980. *Feeling Good*. New York: Signet.

Chambless, D., and T. Ollendick. 2001. Empirically supported psychological interventions: Controversies and evidence. *Annual Review of Psychology* 52: 685–716.

Collins, G. R. 1988. *Christian Counseling: A Comprehensive Guide*. Rev. ed. Dallas: Word.

Copeland, M. E. 2001. *The Depression Workbook*. 2nd ed. Oakland, Calif.: New Harbinger.

Crabb, L. 1977. *Effective Biblical Counseling*. Grand Rapids: Zondervan.

———. 1987. *Understanding People*. Grand Rapids: Zondervan.

———. 1988. *Inside Out*. Colorado Springs, Colo.: NavPress.

———. 1993. *Finding God*. Grand Rapids: Zondervan.

———. 1997. *Connecting*. Nashville: Word.

———. 1999. *The Safest Place on Earth*. Nashville: Word.

———. 2001. *Shattered Dreams*. Colorado Springs, Colo.: WaterBrook.

———. 2002. *The Pressure's Off*. Colorado Springs, Colo.: WaterBrook.

Craighead, W. E., A. B. Hart, L. W. Craighead, and S. S. Ilardi. 2002. Psychosocial treatments for major depressive disorder. In *A Guide to Treatments That Work*, ed. P. E.

Nathan and J. M. Gorman, 245–61. 2nd ed. New York: Oxford University Press.

Craighead, W. E., D. J. Miklowitz, E. Frank, and F. C. Vajk. 2002. Psychosocial treatments for bipolar disorder. In *A Guide to Treatments That Work*, ed. P. E. Nathan and J. M. Gorman, 263–75. 2nd ed. New York: Oxford University Press.

Ellis, A., and R. A. Harper. 1975. *A New Guide to Rational Living*. North Hollywood, Calif.: Wilshire.

Fawcett, J., B. Golden, and N. Rosenfeld. 2000. *New Hope for People with Bipolar Disorder*. Roseville, Calif.: Prima.

Flach, F. F. 1974. *The Secret Strength of Depression*. Philadelphia: Lippincott.

Flynn, M., and D. Gregg. 1993. *Inner Healing*. Downers Grove, Ill.: InterVarsity.

Foster, R. 1978. *Celebration of Discipline*. San Francisco: Harper & Row.

———. 1988. *Celebration of Discipline*. Rev. ed. San Francisco: Harper & Row.

Frances, A., and A. B. First. 1998. *Your Mental Health: A Layman's Guide to the Psychiatrist's Bible*. New York: Scribner.

Garzon, F., and L. Burkett. 2002. Healing of memories: Models, research, future directions. *Journal of Psychology and Christianity* 21: 42–49.

Greenberger, D., and C. A. Padesky. 1995. *Mind over Mood*. New York: Guilford.

Gut, E. 1989. *Productive and Unproductive Depression: Success or Failure of a Vital Process*. New York: Basic.

Hart, A. 1987. *Counseling the Depressed.* Waco: Word.

———. 1993. *Dark Clouds, Silver Linings.* Colorado Springs, Colo.: Focus on the Family.

———. 1995. *Adrenaline and Stress,* Rev. ed.. Dallas: Word.

———. 2001. *Unmasking Male Depression.* Nashville: W Publishing Group.

Hart, A. D., and C. A. Weber. 2002. *Unveiling Depression in Women.* Grand Rapids: Revell.

Hyder, O. Q. 1979. *Shape Up.* Old Tappan, N.J.: Revell.

Jamison, K. R. 1999. *Night Falls Fast: Understanding Suicide.* New York: Knopf.

Johnson, S. L., and R. L. Leahy, eds. 2004. *Psychological Treatments of Bipolar Disorder.* New York: Guilford.

Kennedy, E., and S. C. Charles. 1990. *On Becoming a Counselor.* Expanded ed. New York: Continuum.

Klerman, G. L., M. M. Weissman, B. J. Rounsaville, and E. S. Chevron. 1984. *Interpersonal Psychotherapy of Depression.* New York: Basic.

Klosko, J. S., and W. C. Sanderson. 1999. *Cognitive-Behavioral Treatment of Depression.* Northvale, N.J.: Jason Aronson.

Kruis, J. G. 2000. *Quick Scripture Reference for Counseling.* 3rd ed. Grand Rapids: Baker.

Lam, D. H., S. H. Jones, P. Hayward, and J. A. Bright. 1999. *Cognitive Therapy for Bipolar Disorder: A Therapist's Guide to Concepts, Methods, and Practice.* Chichester, U.K.: Wiley.

Lewinsohn, P. M., R. F. Munoz, M. A. Youngren, and A. M. Zeiss. 1992. *Control Your Depression.* New York: Fireside/Simon and Schuster.

Lloyd-Jones, M. 1965. *Spiritual Depression*. Grand Rapids: Eerdmans.

Lyles, M. R. 2001. Will the real mood stabilizer please stand up? *Christian Counseling Today* 9(3): 60–61.

Maj, M., H. S. Akiskal, J. J. Lopez-Ibor, and N. Sartorius, eds. 2002. *Bipolar Disorder*. New York: Wiley.

Manchester, W. 1983. *The Last Lion: Winston Spencer Churchill*. New York: Dell.

Martell, C. R., M. E. Addis, and N. S. Jacobson. 2001. *Depression in Context: Strategies for Guided Action*. New York: Norton.

McCullough, J. P. 2000. *Treatment of Chronic Depression: Cognitive Behavioral Analysis System for Psychotherapy*. New York: Guilford.

McGrath, E. 1992. *When Feeling Bad Is Good*. New York: Henry Holt.

McGrath, E., G. P. Keita, B. Strickland, and N. F. Russo, eds. 1990. *Women and Depression*. Washington, D.C.: American Psychological Association.

McMinn, M. 1991. *Cognitive Therapy Techniques in Christian Counseling*. Dallas: Word.

Meier, P., S. Aterburn, and F. Minirth. 2001. *Mood Swings*. Nashville: Nelson.

Miklowitz., D. J. 2002. *The Bipolar Disorder Survival Guide*. New York: Guilford.

Miklowitz, D. J., and M. J. Goldstein. 1997. *Bipolar Disorder: A Family-Focused Treatment Approach*. New York: Guilford.

Miller, P. A. 2002. *Quick Scripture Reference for Counseling Women.* Grand Rapids: Baker.

Minirth, F., and P. Meier. 1994. *Happiness is a Choice.* 2nd ed. Grand Rapids: Baker.

Nagel, P. 1983. *Descent from Glory.* New York: Oxford University Press.

National Institute of Mental Health (NIMH). 1999. *The Numbers Count* (NIH Publication No. NIH 99–4584) [online]. Available: http://www.NIMH.NIH.gov/publicat /members.CFM

Newman, C. F., R. L. Leahy, A. T. Beck, N. A. Reilly-Harrington, and L. Gyulai. 2002. *Bipolar Disorder: A Cognitive Therapy Approach.* Washington, D.C.: American Psychological Association.

Ortberg, J. 1998. *Love Beyond Reason: Moving God's Love from Your Head to Your Heart.* Grand Rapids: Zondervan.

———. 2001. *If You Want to Walk on Water, You've Got to Get Out of the Boat.* Grand Rapids: Zondervan.

———. 2002. *The Life You've Always Wanted: Spiritual Disciplines for Ordinary People.* Expanded ed. Grand Rapids: Zondervan.

———. 2003. *Everybody's Normal Till You Get to Know Them.* Grand Rapids: Zondervan.

Owens, V. S. 1993. The dark side of grace. *Christianity Today* (July): 32–35.

Papolos, D., and J. Papolos. 1992. *Overcoming Depression.* Rev. ed. New York: Harper Perennial.

———. 1997. *Overcoming Depression.* 3rd ed. New York: HarperCollins.

———. 1999. *The Bipolar Child.* New York: Broadway Books.

Payne, L. 1991. *Restoring the Christian Soul: Overcoming the Barriers to Completion in Christ through Healing Prayer.* Grand Rapids: Baker.

Persons, J. B., J. Davidson, and M. A. Tompkins. 2001. *Essential Components of Cognitive-Behavior Therapy for Depression.* Washington, D.C.: American Psychological Association.

Podell, R. M., and P. Shimer. 1992. *Contagious Emotions.* New York: Pocket Books.

Propst, L. R. 1988. *Psychotherapy in a Religious Framework: Spirituality in the Emotional Healing Process.* New York: Human Sciences.

Regier, D. A., R. D. A. Hirschfeld, F. K. Goodwin, J. D. Burke Jr., J. B. Lazar, and L. L. Judd. 1988. The NIMH Depression Awareness, Recognition, and Treatment Program: Structure, aims, and scientific basis. *American Journal of Psychiatry* 145: 1351–57.

Robins, C. J., and A. M. Hayes. 1993. An appraisal of cognitive therapy. *Journal of Consulting and Clinical Psychology* 61(2): 205–14.

Rosenthal, N. E. 1993. *Winter Blues: Seasonal Affective Disorder. What It Is and How to Overcome It.* New York: Guilford.

Ross, H. M., and J. Roth. 1990. *The Mood-Control Diet.* New York: Prentice Hall.

Ross, J. 2002. *The Mood Cure.* New York: Viking.

Sanders, R. K., and H. N. Malony. 1985. *Speak Up! Christian Assertiveness.* Philadelphia: Westminster.

Sapsted, A. M. 1990. *Banish Post-Baby Blues.* Wellingborough, Northamptonshire: Thorsons.

Scott, J. 2001. *Overcoming Mood Swings.* New York: New York University Press.

Seamands, D. 1985. *Healing of Memories.* Wheaton: Victor. Republished 2002 as *Redeeming the Past.*

Seligman, M. E. P. 1975. *Helplessness: On Depression, Development, and Death.* San Francisco: Freeman.

———. 1990. *Learned Optimism.* New York: Knopf.

Sider, R. 1993. Winter depression. *Christian Counseling Today* 1(1): 46.

Smedes, L. 1984. *Forgive and Forget.* New York: Harper & Row.

———. 1993. *Shame and Grace.* San Francisco: HarperCollins.

Stamford, B. A., and P. Shimer. 1990. *Fitness without Exercise.* New York: Warner.

Stoll, A. L. 2001. *The Omega-3 Connection.* New York: Simon & Schuster.

Storr, A. 1988. *Solitude: A Return to the Self.* New York: Ballantine.

Sue, D. W., and D. Sue. 2003. *Counseling the Culturally Diverse.* 4th ed. New York: Wiley.

Tan, S. Y. 1987. Cognitive-behavior therapy: A biblical approach and critique. *Journal of Psychology and Theology* 15: 103–12.

———. 1989. Psychopathology and culture: The Asian American context. *Journal of Psychology and Christianity* 8(2): 61–75.

———. 1991. *Lay Counseling: Equipping Christians for a Helping Ministry.* Grand Rapids: Zondervan.

———. 1992. The Holy Spirit and counseling ministries. *The Christian Journal of Psychology and Counseling* 7(3): 8–11.

———. 1996. Religion in clinical practice: Implicit and explicit integration. In *Religion and the Clinical Practice of Psychology,* ed. E. Shafranske, 365–87. Washington, D.C.: American Psychological Association.

———. 2001. Empirically supported treatments. *Journal of Psychology and Christianity* 20: 282–86.

———. 2003. *Rest: Experiencing God's Peace in a Restless World.* Vancouver, B.C.: Regent College.

Tan, S. Y., and N. J. Dong. 2000. Psychotherapy with members of Asian American churches and spiritual traditions. In *Handbook of Psychotherapy and Religious Diversity,* ed. P. S. Richards and A. E. Bergin, 421–44. Washington, D.C.: American Psychological Association.

Tan, S. Y., and D. H. Gregg. 1997. *Disciplines of the Holy Spirit.* Grand Rapids: Zondervan.

Tan, S. Y., and W. B. Johnson. 2004. Cognitive-behavioral approach. In *Spiritually-Oriented Psychotherapy: Contemporary Approaches,* ed. L. Sperry and E. Shafranske. Washington, D.C.: American Psychological Association.

Thomas, B. 1952. *Abraham Lincoln.* New York: Knopf.

Torrey, E. F., and M. B. Knable. 2002. *Surviving Manic Depression.* New York: Basic.

Thurman, C. 1989. *The Lies We Believe.* Nashville: Nelson.

Weissman, M. M., J. C. Markowitz, and G. L. Klerman. 2000. *Comprehensive Guide to Interpersonal Psychotherapy.* New York: Basic.

Whybrow, P., and R. Bahr. 1988. *The Hibernation Response.* New York: Arbor House, William Morrow.

Willard, D. 1988. *The Spirit of the Disciplines.* San Francisco: Harper & Row.

Worthington, E. L., Jr. 2001. *Five Steps to Forgiveness: The Art and Science of Forgiving.* New York: Crown.

———. 2003. *Forgiving and Reconciling: Bridges to Wholeness and Hope.* Downers Grove, Ill.: InterVarsity.

Worthington, E. L., Jr., and S. J. Sandage. 2001. Religion and spirituality. *Psychotherapy* 38: 473–78.

Wright, H. N. 1986. *Self-Talk, Imagery, and Prayer in Counseling.* Waco: Word.

———. 1988. *Beating the Blues.* Ventura, Calif.: Regal.

Siang-Yang Tan teaches in the Graduate School of Psychology at Fuller Theological Seminary. His Ph.D. is from McGill University. He is also senior pastor of First Evangelical Church of Glendale, California.

John Ortberg holds a M.Div. degree and Ph.D. in clinical psychology from Fuller Seminary. The author of *Everybody's Normal Till You Get to Know Them* and *If You Want to Walk on Water, You've Got to Get Out of the Boat*, Ortberg is a pastor at Menlo Park Presbyterian Church in Menlo Park, California.